WE'RE DRIVING OUR KIDS CRAZY
The Shift to Non-Guilt Parenting

by
Arlie Jean Payne

We're Driving Our Kids Crazy

The Shift to Non-Guilt Parenting

Published by

R&E Publishers

P.O. Box 2008
Saratoga, CA 95070
Phone: (408) 866-6303
Fax: (408) 866-0825

I.S.B.N. 0-88247-864-8
Library of Congress 90-50893

Dedicated with grateful appreciation
to my parents and children
with the hope and prayer
that I am more of a plus
than a minus as a link
between generations.

- Jean Payne

INTRODUCTION

We are driving children crazy; then we blame them for their craziness. It may be somewhat comforting that we were driven crazy by our parents who were driven crazy by their parents. It is past time to break the cycle. Our children are in trouble! When they are in trouble, so is our future.

Our children are having babies! They are dropping out of school! They are on drugs! They are fighting gang wars! They are running away from home! They are in correctional institutions! They are committing suicide! Our children are in serious trouble because we, the adults, are driving them crazy! After twenty years of working with parents of preschool children, I have learned that most parents absorb the blame that "society" imposes and feel some guilt if their children don't behave appropriately at all times.

It is important for me to share what I have learned as a mother of five children, with seventeen years difference in ages, and as a director of college parent education programs. As a young parent, searching for ways to resolve the issues in our family, I began to realize how little we are prepared for the intense personal relationships that a family represents. Sharing what I have learned may be one way to absolve the guilt I feel because of ignorance. Too often, we react the way we were reacted to, rather than learn responsible family relationships. It is impossible to change the past, but maybe this book can help make the future for today's children more promising.

Ashley Montague, the well-known anthropologist, said: "It is not evil babies who grow up into evil human beings, but an evil society which turns good babies into disordered adults, and it does so on a regiment of frustration."

Children are born with "stars in their eyes." During the first three months babies are learning whether to trust or mistrust this family they have joined. Those "significant others" will determine their developing self-esteem and whether they will have an optimistic nature.

We are the ones who must assume the responsibility to break the cycle if we are to stop this craziness. We must develop our understanding of how we all grow and learn. It is essential to understand ourselves and how we were raised, how our homes and schools impacted us, and why what we are doing now is not working. We are the models for our children. They will be like us!

It is important to determine what an educated person could be and learn how to provide an environment where our children will be truly educated and grow into effective parents. We need to understand the difference between schooling and education. They are not synonymous. We cannot remain a Nation At Risk and survive the 21st century.

An educated person, by my definition, would recognize the importance of and would be able to gather relevant knowledge, internalize the information at the feeling level, develop the ability to make informed decisions, use anger constructively to resolve conflicts, and move confidently to assume a responsible position in the world community. This might lead to exchanges of the mind and spirit and a transformation of relationships.

In the past, proponents of the traditional college education have claimed a broad liberal arts background would prepare students for effective living. During the past 40 years, the highest percentage of students in the history of our country have received college degrees. How can we measure that impact on this country? The Gross National Product or the salaries of the graduates is often used, but might these sobering statistics be a more accurate gauge?

- Suicide is the second cause of death among teenagers, increasing rapidly in the under 14 year-olds.

- The rate of divorce is tragic and it is impossible to measure the anguish that results.

- Discipline in the classroom and vandalism to our schools and communities are serious problems with devastating effect on morale of teachers.

- Remedial classrooms are a regular part of educational programs with about 25% of our students dropping out of school.

- Many of those drop-outs will be sent to correctional institutions with an annual cost of $25,000-40,000 for each person with little demonstrable success at rehabilitation.

- The prisons cannot hold all the convicted criminals and white-collar crime is constantly being exposed, but maybe not effectively punished.

- The number of pregnancies in the under fifteen age group has been increasing rapidly with abortions the frequent means of birth control.

- The mentally ill, people with alcohol and drug-related problems, including infants born with addiction and birth defects, are national disasters.

- Venereal disease is now found in ten, eleven, and twelve year old children.

- More Americans die on our highways each year than were killed during the Viet Nam war and more than half of the accidents were drug and alcohol related.

- One out of 3-4 girls and 7-10 boys have been sexually abused and approximately 80-90% by someone they know with half of those fathers or step-fathers.

- Obesity is a national problem as the billions spent on dieting aids testifies.

- A small percentage of people vote with the smallest number voting in the last election since 1924.

- Psychologists maintain we develop a limited 3-13% of our potential and the families of the wealthy seem to be as vulnerable as the "disadvantaged."

It is hard to say that a college education is making a difference. Whose responsibility is it to address these issues? Can and should education prepare people for competent and confident living?

Have Social Studies produced responsible involvement in the social process?

Have Economic classes prepared people for effective money management, including planning and saving for college for children and their retirement?

Have people who have taken Political Science classes voted more often and more knowledgeably than ones who have not?

Do people who have taken Communication classes have improved listening skills, deal with anger more constructively with less divorce?

Do Psychology graduates understand and relate to people more honestly and effectively with less mental illness?

Aldous Huxley has said, "What a great gulf separates the knowledge of the obvious from the actual living of it. And oh, the difficulties in crossing the gulf! I perceive now that the real charm of the intellectual life—the life devoted to erudition, to scientific research, to philosophy, to aesthetics, to criticism—is its easiness. It's incomparably easier to know a lot, say, about the history of art and to have profound ideas about metaphysics and sociology than to know personally and intuitively a lot about one's fellow and to have satisfactory relations with one's friends and lovers, one's wife and children. Living is much more difficult than Sanskrit or Chemistry or Economics."

Behavioral changes have not occurred as a result of knowledge. When a woman with a Master's Degree in Child Growth and Development was asked about its impact on her children, she said, "At the end of the day when the children are tired and I am tired, I react rather than do what I know I should." Our knowledge is not internalized so that we act appropriately. Too often, we are still reacting to our children as we were reacted to by our parents, no matter how often we promised ourselves we wouldn't do that when we had children.

How do we internalize knowledge so it does make a difference in the way we live? Are educators responsible? If educators are not, who is? The parents are usually blamed. Teachers have had five years of college education learning how to teach and they have a curriculum developed by experts to follow yet education is under much criticism. Teachers tend to blame the parents who have had no education for parenthood and no curriculum to follow (if there could be a curriculum).

Do people need education before parenthood or after they become parents or both? We need certification or licenses for almost everything else we do. Who would educate the parents and could or should they be certified? If a goal of education would be to educate our children for living with people would they be more successful parents when they grew up?

As cause and effect have been researched, there is a developing realization that clues for making that crucial difference may be found in what happens during the first five years of life. Researchers indicate that intellectual development, social attitudes, personality traits, and attitudes toward learning develop during the years before school, but that we have not been successful at understanding ways to influence and enhance that learning. Children have an unbelievable and magical ability to learn. Language is the most complex learning of all and children learn it more successfully (unless adults interfere with the process) than teachers with college degrees have been able to teach academic subjects in school. Would Family Studies be the answer? We haven't had the greatest success teaching reading. Could we develop Family Studies courses that would make measurable behavioral changes?

Because the family is such a personal, subjective, developing kind of learning, can it be taught? Is there a relationship between the family and mental illness, school drop-outs, delinquency, alcoholism, teenage pregnancy, child abuse, divorce? If so, what is the educational institution's responsibility? How have the schools contributed to these problems? Should Child Growth and Development and Parenting classes be required? If not in the schools, how are we going to learn? Who will teach? How? When?

Should Family Studies have at least equal emphasis as traditional courses that have "answers" such as English, Chemistry, or Math?

Is it a vocation that is as important as Auto Mechanics, Cosmetology, and Nursing?

It is important to move away from "doing to" our children and assume the responsibility to model for our children. I am responsible for me and how I relate to all.

Everyone lives in the Family of Man. Everyone deserves the opportunity to develop the knowledge and skills to live confidently, competently in that Family. It is essential to model self-actualizing growth and maturity for our children. That will allow them to feel good about themselves and to want to cooperate and empathize with others.

Can we find ways to stop driving our children crazy?

Can we keep the "stars in their eyes?"

Table of Contents

We Drive Our Kids Crazy Unless We Live Happily Ever After

"And they lived happily ever after!" Thus the fairy tale ends and deep down inside each of us *know* we will grow up to fall in love, living happily ever after. Certainly, I expected to fall in love, get married, and live happily ever after.

It had not occurred to me to explore likes and dislikes, values and priorities, hopes and goals before marriage. For instance, I had grown up in a Christian family. My grandfather was a Methodist minister, I have my cradle roll certificate and as I grew up, went to all church related activities, including Sunday School, youth group, camp, and singing in the choir. I believed we were a Christian nation so everyone was a Christian. I knew my future husband liked my grandfather, but we never discussed religion before marriage. It was devastating for me to learn our religious differences as we lived within our marriage. How was I possibly going to raise our children with the differences I was discovering? I didn't have the skills to resolve them.

My mother died while I was in high school and as a result, when I was to be married, many relatives and friends felt it necessary to discuss the "facts of life". There certainly wasn't much agreement on what those facts were. My grandmother wanted me to think about my fiance's family. I can remember resenting the intrusion and reacting huffily, "Grandma, I'm not marrying his family!" Without ever consciously thinking about it, I was sure that we were going to live happily ever after.

It is only in retrospect that I can begin to reconstruct the naivete that I went into marriage.

Then we were expecting our first child. Early in the pregnancy, my husband brought home a parent's manual. I eagerly read it and was very surprised to learn that toilet training should wait until the child was "ready". At that time, most were setting babies on wee little cup-sized pots and groaning about the "ordeal" of toilet training.

I recognized immediately that I didn't know the first thing about babies and systematically began reading everything possible. Our first child was born! I gradually became uncomfortable with some other differences in our attitudes that was surfacing. My husband was not at all interested and during World War II we were often apart. After all, Dad was supposed to earn the living and Mom was supposed to raise the children.

I found myself struggling between the wife I wanted to be (we two were to be one) and the mother I wanted to be to our son and the ambivalence and confusion I was feeling. I was completely unable to communicate these feelings to my husband in a way that generated discussion.

I began to experience the intensity of the conflicts couples can have without finding a successful method of verbalizing them. Marriage and family became a painful dilemma much of the time rather than the joy I could envision it to be. I knew that I truly loved my husband and I knew that I thoroughly loved my children and my responsibilities for our home. The times that were joyous were so satisfying and I wanted to find a way to have a joyful communicating family and could not figure out a way to make it happen.

In order to quit driving children crazy, it is essential for the husband and wife to achieve joyful communication respecting each other's right to be themselves but learning to communicate for a *lasting* relationship during the early years of marriage when both are eager to make it work.

We have to learn it is necessary to share our likes and dislikes, value and priorities, hopes and goals coming to some common agreement that allows for the individual to be respected but recognizes the importance of the relationship. This can be an exciting challenge if both come in to the relationship understanding the complexities of integrating into a family. Our divorce rate suggests that doesn't happen very often.

Often a young couple will say, "but we never quarrel." If that is because they started right away working hard at learning where the different expectations were and resolving and accepting them without an angry exchange, then I would guess they were an exceptional couple.

More often, it means that each is sublimating their differences and avoiding discussing them. Gradually a wall is built of subjects that it isn't safe to discuss. Unless they learn how to talk about these differences, the burden becomes unbearable in ten—twenty—thirty years. That is why friends are shocked when such a couple gets a divorce. There is nothing they can share and the burden of not being free to be oneself is too much to bear any longer. But quarreling often doesn't end in resolving differences either. We need to learn how to resolve differences with warmth and compassion.

As young marrieds, it is important to ask these questions. Can I talk to my spouse about anything and everything and expect an effort to understand and support me? Can my partner expect the same from me? (During a community discussion of sex education, I heard one mother argue against inviting a speaker who had a reputation for straight talk with teenagers, indicating he would talk to teenagers about things she couldn't even talk to her husband about.) Can we accept our right to be different but daily work towards achieving mutual support and empathy? Are we open with our partners?

What does openness mean? Another word that might help define this word is authentic. We want to be sure that as often as possible our words match our feelings and we don't pretend to be something we are not. It is important, I believe, to learn how to share negative as well as positive feelings with people who are close to us. Many misunderstandings are avoided if we can share our feelings and be sure that each understands what the other is meaning! A solid relationship can be built if we can find ways to talk about what makes us angry, hurt, sad, uncomfortable and work them out so our relationship can be strengthened.

After each encounter there should be greater warmth toward each other. Kiss and make-up in such a way that the current issue is resolved rather than buried.

It is important not to talk about those intimate exchanges with anyone else. Members of the family need to be able to trust that the private things that happen between them will not be shared with others.

A dilemma arises when one partner has always discussed a wide variety of subjects easily with others, which often means she came from a family that was open and free. The one partner may feel betrayed if it is discovered that the spouse is able to discuss a subject that he has never been comfortable talking to *anyone* about.

I think sex is one of these subjects. One partner may be comfortable talking about sexual attitudes and relationships. The other partner may be most uncomfortable and may feel betrayed, even though nothing of personal intimacy was shared. If we can learn to be sensitive to how another is feeling, then we are able to deal openly with those feelings. If we aren't aware of these differences, it can build resentments and interfere in future communications.

Openness will lead to happier, more intimate relationships with people.

When we are revealing, it will diminish the relationship. It is possible to talk about relationships and their importance without sharing the very personal ways we relate to some particular person.

It takes courage to be intimate if we have never done it. It is essential to step out with courage to build the husband-wife relationship in open sharing ways, if we are to become parents that will not drive each other and our children crazy.

It is important to know that a child's self-esteem is directly related by how parents relate to each other and to their children. We need to explore ways to relate to people in positive ways that enhance self-esteem. The same rules apply to relationships with children. Often we talk to and about our children in ways we would not talk about anyone else and even do it in front of them. For example, sometimes children, because of their limited understanding, say things that are funny to us. Let us get permission to share those wonderfully amusing anecdotes before we do.

Years ago Saturday Night Live had an episode that the parents in our program shared with me. The writer's 12 year old son had commented to his dad that he didn't treat his children the way he treated his friends. The writer developed a script where people treated their guests like they did their children. When they arrived for the evening, the hosts demanded that they wipe their feet before they came in, wash their hands before eating, clean up their plate in order to have dessert. The parents said they laughed so hard when they saw that episode but all the time they were hurting inside because it graphically illustrated the truth.

It is possible to explore ways to be intimate without revealing personal intimacy. We can explore methods to clarify our values and to establish priorities. I need to be comfortable talking about sex myself before I can talk with my children in a way that won't convey embarrassment or shame. Talking with others regarding values and how to live them will make us more comfortable. Often, in matters sexual, it takes practice to use accurate terms for bodily functions. (A coach I once knew was sent to a summer school session to learn about teaching sex education in the school. He said it took all summer for the class to become comfortable using proper terms.)

Becoming aware of messages given and values one hopes to pass on is worthwhile. That is different than sharing the personal intimacies one has with one's partner. It can also be uncomfortable if someone shares a private matter with the expectation that you also share the same kind of detail with them.

Unless a husband and wife work daily at sharing and understanding, developing a relationship that is open and empathetic, one partner may feel a desperate need to have someone to talk with that will offer empathy and understanding. In desperation there will be a search for *someone* to confide in at the expense of the marriage relationship.

For protection of the marriage and family, it is essential to make every effort to communicate in positive life-sustaining ways that will lead to joyful family relationships. Men will probably have to become more aware of the need for intimate communication since our society has emphasized the "macho" silent male image.

The most important way we can prevent craziness in our children, is to have a loving husband-wife relationship. It should be a top priority. It may mean putting courtship time first. We often neglect courting once the marriage is consummated. Often expense money for "dating" our mates is lost when we start mortgage payments. We might be together to celebrate burning the mortgage papers, if we did make dating our partners a top priority.

Maybe if we put continuing time for courtship first, we may provide our children with the parents they need. As we learn to treat each other with respect, resolving conflicts, demonstrating warm compassionate relationships, we are becoming parents that won't drive our children crazy.

We Drive Our Kids Crazy Unless We Resolve Conflict

"What shall we do? My husband and I can't agree on how to raise our kids!" was a complaint I heard frequently as a director of parent education. This is a perplexing challenge for many young parents today.

When I was developing the marriage role questionaire at the end of this chapter, I showed it to some friends at a dinner party. The older men (my age) thought it would take all the romance out of young love. Their wives and the young people thought it would be most helpful.

Society puts young people in a double bind. On the one hand, it says, " *Anyone* can babysit!" There is another strong message that parents internalize, "It's all the parents' fault if children don't turn out 'right'!"

There is little preparation for parenthood. (Anyone can babysit!) Pre-school and child care-givers often receive minimum wages. (You don't need to know much to take care of preschoolers!) What a tragic misunderstanding of the importance of these very critical years before school.

As a result, young people become parents without any preparation and with little idea of what parenthood involves. Many have moved away from their families. Years ago, there were large families and the older children had experience with the younger and the younger children gained experience with little nieces and nephews. Today's young parents haven't had much opportunity to have contact with very young children, let alone responsibility for them.

Parents of many young couples had small families with children fairly close in ages. Many new parents have never even held a new baby until they hold their own. That experience can provide a mixture of fear and awe.

The doctor that delivered the baby had to have extensive preparation, even though for thousands of years, babies came naturally. The nurses spent years in school, even the dad that drives the new family home from the hospital had to have a driver's license. The new parents with the most important responsibility of all has had very little preparation.

It is believed that everyone knows how to parent, that it just comes instinctively. (The parent education program in the community colleges spent time fighting for its life because college administrators, state board members, and legislators didn't believe it necessary. The program was ousted from some churches because parishioners didn't want the "state telling anyone how to parent".)

The parents usually have developed a few notions about how "they" are going to raise "their" children. ("I'm sure not going to let my kids do that.") The first baby arrives and neither parent had any idea that it was going to be like *this*!

A baby will make our family complete (the pretty nursery, the baby to cuddle) is the first myth that impacts with shocking explosion. What really happens? The baby cries when it is supposed to be sleeping, quite often when the parents are making love! That is an effective way to develop a triangle relationship and is more common than realized! Spitting up when eating, wanting to play in the middle of the night, fussing all during your dinner is routine behavior for wee ones.

It's a relentless 24 hour day, 7 day a week job with no respite! Exhaustion often results! Parents begin to realize that this "family" idea isn't at all what was expected. They begin to develop more respect for what their parents went through, but it is just the beginning.

Instead of realizing that child rearing is a complex, challenging task that has stumped the experts, the confused young parents often react..."Anyone can babysit! What is the matter with me?"

When two people fall in love, romance and hormones take over and there is not much thought given to what marriage is all about. Rarely is serious attention given to child-rearing methods. Often there is no discussion until that new baby is conceived.

There has been a strong movement toward childbirth education, which deals with preparation for the birth. As a parent educator, I was often asked to speak to childbirth groups regarding the period after the baby arrives. I found that the main response was from the couples who already had children. They were very interested and had many questions. The first time expectant parents seem to find it difficult to relate to the reality of life after birth. They just wanted to get through childbirth. They seemed to believe the future would take care of itself.

When the new baby arrives, the parents' different attitudes regarding family issues begin to surface. They are usually reacting the way their parents reacted to them, which, of course, is rarely the same since no two families are alike. Ideas regarding all family issues will surface, including ones that heretofore they thought had been resolved, such as religion. Each person was disciplined differently for different behaviors.

We treat our children the way we were treated even though we promised ourselves when we were growing up that we would never do that when we had kids. I believe this can be the basis for the Old Testament statement "visiting the iniquity of fathers upon children upon the third and fourth generation" Numbers 14-18. It is important to learn how children learn and how to cooperate with that learning and stop reacting in the way to which we were reacted.

When it becomes apparent there are basic differences, parents might make an effort to present an united front. After all, that is what "society" says should happen, isn't it?

If attitudes and beliefs can be discussed, genuine understanding and agreement reached with both parents feeling comfortable using agreed upon approaches, great, it minimizes the problem. However, that kind of agreement is rare. It soon becomes apparent that there are unresolved basic differences and then the society imposed cliche, "parents should present an united front" rears its ugly head and the disagreements become intense. An effort may be made to compromise. Each figures his/her way is right. After all, that is the way they were raised and they turned out all right. They have to defend their upbringing because otherwise it would suggest that their parents failed. That would be most damaging to their own self-esteem, which is at a low ebb anyway at threatening times.

Child-rearing methods are often argued vehemently without resolving differences or are never talked out so that resentments smolder. What preparation have any of us had for sharing our feelings and resolving differences? If a compromise is reached, each is likely to have reservations about it. This leads to feelings of guilt. If they try to act on those compromises, it is apt not to work. Children seem to have a built-in radar which enables them to sense the underlying emotions that affect their parents so there is no practicality in pretense.

Although I believed in an united front as a young parent, I gradually became aware that it wasn't working. As I tried to evaluate why, I decided it couldn't work without a great deal of understanding and effort. Each parent has grown up with different family experiences that influence attitudes, beliefs, and behaviors. These usually are not conscious and certainly not easily recognized, explored, and changed.

From early childhood, we have heard the fairy tale that someday a prince (or princess) will come, ending with, "And they lived happily ever after," and we believed it. Courtship love is exciting, blind, and usually quite selfish. (I love her because she makes me feel so good.)

No matter how close a family one has, it doesn't prepare one for marriage, although a family who models positive loving relationships is a solid plus. We expect that our marriage will be like our parent's if their marriage is a good one and that our marriage will never be like our parent's if their's was a bad relationship. Social messages such as "togetherness" or "you two shall become one" or "the wife should submit to the husband" complicate attitudes regarding relationships.

The triangle that a new baby brings is supremely complex. The idea that there can be such a triangle is shocking. How can one be jealous of a new baby! It does happen!

Think of how eagerly a husband might be looking forward to renewing a sexual relationship after abstention during the birth of the child. Then imagine how frustrating it can be to have that new wee one interfere. There is some indication that the baby does have an awareness, whether sensitivity to the scent or a psychic bond is not known. It *is* known that new babies often interrupt sexual activity. Imagine how the new mother must be torn between meeting the baby's needs and responding to her husband and her own needs! This triangle, if recognized, can be joked about, "there he goes again."

A relationship takes time to build; imposing a father-mother relationship too soon can jeopardize the marriage unless feelings are explored openly and parental roles are understood. Learning how to maintain the husband-wife relationships while building effective father-mother relationships is a complex but essential activity. Too often young parents get caught up in the very busy parenting schedules and responsibilities, neglecting to continue the vital "courting" that is necessary to maintain the husband/wife relationship. That positive relationship is absolutely the most important gift parents can give their children.

This means it is necessary to examine alternative family structures. Each family is different. Some families had quite authoritarian fathers, while other families were fairly democratic. Although our form of government has been democratic for numbers of generations, the Civil Right's movement has given new insights into equal rights. While there has been a growing recognition that everyone, including children, have rights and the need for respect, there often has been no model to follow, and each family has had to struggle to define the new parental roles.

This has been a slow, agonizing process and for the most part a subconscious one. Parents groping to build new roles are insecure and children reflect these feelings. The old adage, "a child should be seen and not heard," is recognized as outdated.

If we are to "live happily ever after" we must examine our family backgrounds and our parents' roles. The economic, social, cultural, racial, and religious attitudes of our parents determine, more than we are aware, our attitudes until we consciously search for and assess them. Because these attitudes have not been the same for the husband and the wife, it is important to appraise them. Close personal relationships need to be defined in terms of current needs and responsibilities rather than in obsolete roles imposed on us by the past. When these roles are left to chance they can deteriorate into a negative impact on the marriage.

A young woman told our toddler discussion group that her husband served her breakfast in bed. The others, very impressed, wanted to know how she was able to get that to happen. During our discussion, we decided it might be because his father had served his mother breakfast in bed. She confided that she hadn't told him it wasn't necessary. Breakfast in bed would be an easy adjustment to make, but what if *her* father had served *her* mother breakfast in bed and her husband had never heard of such a "ridiculous idea"?

I asked if she would like to be like his mother.

"Goodness, no, she is a terrible hypochondriac! His father waits on her all the time. None of us ever dare ask her how she feels, because she will tell us in great detail!"

"Would you like to be like your mother?"

"Oh, yes, she is so capable and well-organized."

"Would you like your husband to be like your father?"

"Oh, no, he has to ask Mom about everything." Suddenly, this young women had an important insight, exclaiming, "Goodness! I had better not let him serve me breakfast in bed or I might become like his mother."

Consider what might happen if a husband's father handled the money and the wife's mother handled the money; each might expect to be the money manager. What if *his* mother and *her* father managed the budget. There might be no management at all, each expecting the other partner to be responsible. Learning how to share that important but divisive function is a major challenge. Certainly, money is recognized as a major problem in marriage.

Discussion of the partner's roles can enlighten. If it is not discussed, resentments smolder, usually without either partner being aware of the cause. Think how upset a wife might be if her father took the family out to eat every Friday night to give his wife a break from cooking but his family never went out to eat except in emergencies. Every Friday night his wife might be expecting to go out for dinner and be terribly disappointed if he doesn't suggest it. He might wonder why every Friday night his wife is so upset. She doesn't say anything, because she believes it should be his idea and it would spoil it if *she* suggested it. He hasn't the faintest idea of why his wife is so depressed every Friday night.

The positive way to prevent resentments and to arrive at an united front would be to discuss openly and often the role of each. When disagreements surface, the first question can be, "What did our parents do?" Then you can discuss how you want to deal with that kind of situation in your family; thus respect and responsibility is achieved.

After this type of discussion, one young woman exclaimed, "That is why neither of us ever lock the house at night!" When she thought about it, his mother had always locked up at night and her father always had. Each expected the other to do it. Now a conscious decision could be made regarding whose task it would be, and they wouldn't have to get up, after retiring at night, to lock the door.

Often couples are not aware enough of these influences to discuss them. It isn't easy to resolve conflicts that arise, since resolving conflicts isn't a skill successfully taught in our families and schools. (Just look at the divorce rate.) Our differences can cause either explosions or feelings hidden deep inside leading to unexpressed anger that has to come out some way, often not related to current issues.

The guilt becomes intense because we are *supposed* to present an united front. This "united" front leads to frustration and resentment that can come out in negative, critical attitudes toward the children and the partner, or in hidden deep reactions within, manifesting itself in stress-related illness, such as ulcers or arthritis. Children are aware that something is amiss, and their awareness adds to their confusion and self-doubt, which causes them to act out their feelings in negative ways, causing more conflict in the family.

It seems to me, a more healthy way would be to respect the parents' right to react to the children in their own ways. I feel there are advantages to this. First of all, parents would be less apt to feel defensive about how to relate to their children. They wouldn't have to defend their right to relate to their own children in their own fashion. It would eliminate an area of conflict between the parents and as most of us have a great deal to learn about resolving conflicts, we want to eliminate as many as possible.

It would also free parents to be open to explore new ideas if it is not necessary to defend their own.

It was with great relief that I have found support for my convictions. I always feel a little more secure when I find an "authority" supporting ideas I have developed in the "school of hard knocks". Dr. Murray Bowen, Professor of Psychiatry in the Georgetown University School of Medicine at the time I was struggling with understanding the united front issue, presented an additional advantage. He believed that children with separate relationships with each of their parents are in a better position to know men from relating to their fathers and to know women from relating to their mothers. I liked that and wished I had thought of it.

Sometimes the mother becomes the family interpreter which can diminish total family interaction. From childhood, it has been acceptable for little girls to show feelings while little boys are encouraged to hide them. ("Don't cry, take it like a man.") Too often, it is the mother who is concerned about the family, reads the family magazines and books, and develops a greater understanding of relationships. She becomes the "director" of the way a family is to relate. This may prevent the rest of the members from finding ways to relate in their individual ways. It makes it even easier for the father to withdraw from active involvement in the family since society has already absolved him from much of the responsibility. He is supposed to earn the money to support the family, although many moms have added working outside the home to their many responsibilities.

Another important consideration, concerns the feeling of the child when two "giants" unite (as it might appear,) against the child. (Think of the additional trauma of those two "giants" uniting with the school. What overwhelming odds!) It makes the child feel very vulnerable. I believe children need to know that *someone* will *always* be *for* them. A spunky child may use ingenuity to fight the system, another may simply give up. Either way, they are losing trust and collecting anger. Neither position contributes to positive self-esteem. The parents also suffer when there are antagonistic feelings. They *want* to be good parents. They also need to feel good about themselves.

An honest relationship is more productive than a negotiated pretense at an united front and children can accept differences between parents if the parents respect each other in their agreement to disagree. Insights shared, conflicts resolved, differences allowed and accepted can lead toward supportive family relationships. Such relationships are not easily achieved and often involves painful soul-searching plus the courage to share and listen.

I am responsible for the way I relate to children, I am *not* responsible for the way my husband relates to children, unless there is abuse, which makes it necessary to insist on counseling. I wish I had learned all this before my children arrived.

When we are able to develop mature relationships, we find ourselves moving toward an unity that isn't forced.

We need to learn to recognize our feelings and to explore causes for our angers and resentments and then to discuss them with people in open, positive ways. When we can accomplish this, we will be able to relate to our children honestly and lovingly, rather than subjectively falling back on obsolete inherited patterns in moments of stress. We will move from reacting as we were reacted to, to acting thoughtfully, based on the needs of our children.

The following questionaire can give an idea of ways to examine past patterns and roles of parents. There is no right or wrong—just differences.

What part of the country did your parents grow up?

What cultural and regional patterns existed?

Did they live on a farm, in a suburb, or a city?

How did that environment affect their lifestyle?

Did they rent an apartment, home, or own their home?

Did your parents carry life and health insurance?

Did they actively plan for retirement?

Did your parents quarrel openly? Often? What about?

How did they resolve their differences?

Did your parents attend church? How often?

What were their religious beliefs? Did they agree?

Was there a budget? Who was responsible for it?

Who did the grocery shopping? Clothing? Household?

How did they celebrate Christmas? Where?

When were gifts opened?

How often did they eat out? Restaurant? Drive-in?

Did your mother work outside the home?

How did your parents entertain? Casually? Formally?

How many children were in the family?

What were their age differences?

How were the household tasks shared?

How were they assigned?

Was the home maintained neatly and regularly?

Was outside help hired? What for?

Did your parents smoke? Heavily?

Was your mother/father in good health?

What were their favorite forms of recreation?

How frequently did they play?

Did they include the children?

How important were sports? To mother? To father?

What were their hobbies?

What were their attitudes toward education?

Did they save for college education?

What were attitudes regarding racial differences?

What were attitudes toward religious differences?

How were each involved in child rearing?

Who assumed major responsibility for discipline?

How did they discipline? What for?

Who made most of the decisions? How?

Did your father open the car door for your mother?

Did he hold the chair for her at the table?

Was thanks said for the food?

Did you eat meals together? Breakfast? Dinner?

Were meals formal? Informal?

Was there discussion at the table? What about?

Were meals leisurely or over quickly? Fun?

Did your parents show affection and if so, how?

What kind of activities were shared with each other?

What kind of activities were shared with the children?

Who waited up for the children to come in at night?

Who did lock the doors at night?

Do these questions suggest other issues in your relationships that it would be helpful to discuss?

The differences can be discussed and an awareness of where resentments could develop may be discerned. Thoughtful consideration of the options for your developing family can be determined. When conflict develops, first ask each other how each of your parents might have handled it. This would give clues as to whether you are reacting out of your past. Discussion of what is best for your family can ensue and then positive action taken.

Marriage is a continuing challenging relationship. How it develops is determined by your understanding of yourselves, your understanding of how children learn, and each partner's willingness to assume responsibility to learn successful communication skills. Maybe if we work daily at it, with a nightly discussion regarding how each feels regarding the happenings of the day, (noting both the positive and the not so positive) and what can be done to deal constructively with the negative issues; we can model relationships that will lead to happy growth and development of the family. We must model for our children caring constructive relationships. The best thing we can give our children is two parents who very obviously like, respect, and enjoy each other.

If we can establish satisfying relationships in our family, we won't be driving our children crazy. Most importantly, maybe we can build a happy satisfying growing marriage where we live happily ever after 'till death do us part!"

We Drive Our Kids Crazy Unless We Create A Climate For Learning

I wanted to become a teacher from the time I was a small child. I taught at the junior high school level. While teaching those ages, I was concerned because, some of the students were not achieving much and I anguished over ways to make a difference when I had them less than an hour a day. I decided that something should have been done long before they reached junior high school.

Later, I taught kindergarten. Children came in excited and eager to learn and because of the earlier experience with junior high, I looked for answers at a beginning level.

As I looked for ways to make that difference, I realized as the year progressed, that some children would not be ready for what would be expected of them when they were in the first grade. Again, each spring I would be in anguish as I tried to decide which would be most devastating, repeating kindergarten which suggests failure (since the parents interpreted it as "flunking play") or promotion to first grade where I could anticipate certain failure. I was able to follow some of the children as they progressed through school which verified my anticipation of failure.

It was at that time I realized that something happened between kindergarten and junior high school that was destructive.

It has been nearly fifty years since that time and we are very slow at finding ways to "win the losers".

We drive children crazy when we don't allow them to learn *what they need* to learn *when they need* to learn it. Whenever we teach children something they could have "discovered" or "invented" for themselves, we keep them from understanding it. Our responsibility is to provide an environment both at home and at school where children can "discover" for themselves.

Tolstoy recognized the importance of learning during the early years of life: "Was it not then that I acquired all that now sustains me? And I gained so much and so quickly that during the rest of my life I did not acquire a hundredth part of it. From myself as a five-year-old to myself as I now am there is only a step. The distance between myself as an infant and myself at five years is tremendous." And Tolstoy lived many years before all the recent corroborative research.

Researchers such as Burton White, Keith Osborne, David Elkind, Earl Kelley, Jerome Kagan, and Benjamin Bloom recognized the importance of the early years some time ago. They are among the many who spent years researching how very young children learn and grow and develop. Not only intellectual development, but personality traits, and social attitudes are rapidly developing in the years before five.

Adler had suggested that life decisions were made during those very early years. I had a difficult time comprehending that until Chuck, my brother, had a heart attack at age 49. He was a college basketball coach, always competing. After surgery, he was taken to the intensive care room. When I had an opportunity to see him during a brief visit that was allowed each hour, he told me that he was going to get out of that recovery room faster than anyone ever had. I scolded that he wasn't on the basketball court so he did *not* need to be the first.

"Oh, yes I do, because I am the hundredth boy," was his reply.

Not understanding, I asked what did he mean by he was the hundredth boy.

"Don't you remember the poem Mother used to read? She would lift me up in her arms and read that poem," he queried.

I vaguely remembered a poem where ninety-nine boys would achieve in a nondescript way BUT the hundredth boy would achieve in a spectacular way. I was amazed! After his recovery, I asked him about that incident and he had no memory of that conversation. Evidently, his subconscious was talking for him in that half waking state after surgery. That certainly confirmed for me the importance of the early years. It was easy to identify my competitive brother with the hundredth boy.

I think we would be dumfounded to learn what children are actually learning from us. I read that the brick-building industry reported that the American people preferred brick houses even though they cost more and would burn. I was astounded to learn that they gave credit to the story of the Three Little Pigs. Remember? The big bad wolf couldn't blow the brick house down. I can't count the number of times that I have read that story to children, but, not once, did I think that I was teaching those children that brick homes were best or that they would still believe it when they were grown. I know that I am regularly amazed when I listen carefully to children's ideas and insights.

In today's haste to be sure that children learn as much as possible as soon as possible, there is some confusion as to the difference between intellectual development and academic achievement. The dictionary defines intellectual as: the power or faculty of knowing, reasoning, judging, comprehending." Academic is defined: "conforming to scholastic traditions or rules, theoretical and not expected to produce a practical result."

Academic is generally interpreted to mean schooling, teaching the "basics" of reading, writing, and arithmetic. It is important to distinguish the difference in order to understand how learning takes place and to avoid pressure on children, programming them for failure. We have learned much about learning, self-esteem, and the importance of the early years, but we have been very slow at translating it into successful programs in our homes and schools. We *are* driving children crazy!

Benjamin Bloom has demonstrated with disadvantaged children that 95-97% of our children can *master* (yes, he uses the word master) what we believe it is important for them to know. In order to accomplish this, we have to pay attention to two issues. The affective climate should be such that children love to be there, feel cared for, respected, and appreciated. Secondly, that we start where the children are in their development, not where the school system has expected them to be. It is necessary to adapt the system to individual children's needs rather than expect the children to adapt to the system, which is, too often, the current policy. Anxiety is the enemy of intelligence, we have to keep the learning centers relaxed and fun.

The research that Bloom did years ago indicated that more than half of the intellectual development takes place during the preschool years, before formal schooling takes place. Too often, we want to rush in and provide a structure to teach the "basics" to young children, interfering with their natural ability to learn.

Parents often say to preschool teachers that they want their children to learn to read. They have already learned the alphabet on Sesame Street; but they must learn how to listen, the children aren't hearing what they say. Children have an amazing ability to develop the concepts they need without structured academic (school-like) activities. This development is a vitally important prerequisite for successful reading.

Children are the most intensive listeners of all. They also learn very early when it is convenient not to listen. Often we don't listen to them. If a child has to ask questions frequently over and over, we need to examine our own behavior. I often suggest to parents who complain about the incessant talking of those new little talkers, that they set a timer. Tell the child that when the timer goes off you will stop and do what they want until the timer goes off again. It is a great way to be sure that you spend adequate time with them and the child will learn that her "turn" will come.

When our middle daughter was small, I was stirring something at the stove and my mind must have been a million miles away. I "came to" when I heard that three year old say: "What's the matter, Mommie, you used to listen when I talk?" If children are not listening to us, it is important to examine our own behavior to see if we are listening when they talk.

Burton White in his research at Harvard University discovered that attitudes toward learning are developed by age two. We must appreciate the importance of the first few years of life and realize how much learning is taking place that will impact the rest of their lives.

Intellectual development takes place without the benefit of the traditional three "r's" and reading is just one of those "basics" (I'll admit a most valuable one when they are ready.) Reading should be offered at the most efficient time for the child. We have learned, for example, that toilet training will take place more effectively when it is introduced at the time the child is able to recognize and control what his body is telling him. There are a number of important physical, social, and intellectual developments that need to take place before reading is introduced and they occur at different times for different children.

Some children may be ready to learn to read most efficiently at five or younger and they will pick it up so easily that the parents don't know how it happened. Other just as bright children may not reach the efficient time to develop reading until they are seven or older. When they are expected to learn something for which they are not ready, it can be damaging to self-esteem. One-hundred and eighty days in the "slow" reading group can be devastating! When children have to struggle unsuccessfully to learn something, it affects self-esteem. When they try hard and don't succeed they often quit trying. Successful learning is satisfying and fun! Achievement reinforces self-esteem.

It is most important for children to read their world which they do well from the moment of birth. When the appropriate time to learn to read arrives, it will be meaningful. Children from disadvantaged environments (not necessarily economically underprivileged) may need a great many positive experiences before they are offered reading, regardless of age, because children have to believe they can learn, before they will learn.

Many of us have scolded and punished (verbally or physically abused) children until children react in rebellious and non-cooperative ways. Now that I am older and have learned so much about those important early years, I am miserable when I am in public and see adults jerk and yell at children trying to impose obedience. I want to interfere but I haven't figured a way to do it effectively. None of us feel good about ourselves or feel like cooperating when we have been scolded. Children feel the same way we feel in similar circumstances.

We need to treat them as we would like to be treated.

If they have not been allowed to explore their world when they began to creep and toddle, they may have learned "you get in trouble when you learn and adults get in the way." That attitude will have to change before they can succeed in school.

Children's language development is the most complex task of their lifetime. They learn language much more successfully than we have taught reading. Maybe it is because *they* are in charge of their language development. It is often when adults interfere with language development that problems occur.

When that wee one says, "I eated my lunch", he is telling us he knows sentence structure, he knows one adds "ed" to get past tense, but hasn't yet learned there are some exceptions to that rule. We thought we taught grammar in school!

"It is frightening to think that an enormous number of grammatical forms are poured over the poor head of the young child," says Chukovsky, the sensitive Russian poet. "And he, as if it were nothing at all, adjusts to all this chaos, constantly sorting out into rubrics the disorderly elements of the words he hears, without noticing as he does this, his gigantic effort. If an adult had to master so many grammatical rules within so short a time, his head would surely burst—a mass of rules mastered so lightly and so freely by the two-year-old 'linguist'. The labor he performs at this age is astonishing enough, but even more amazing and unparalleled is the ease with which he does it. In truth, the young child is the hardest toiler in our planet. Fortunately, he does not even suspect this."

Maybe we are interfering with their natural ability to learn!

Our job as parents and teachers is to take our clues from our children. They will let us know what and when they are ready to learn. Our responsibility is to create the opportunity and cooperate with their interests. We must quit imposing our notions of what they *should* be learning and create an environment where they learn because it is so exciting.

We need to keep the "stars in their eyes!"

It is vital to arrange a system where children will have much to say about what they want to learn and when to learn it. Sixth grade children can be most helpful when working with children of primary age. Having three or four age levels in each classroom would require individual attention with the older helping the younger. We will have to be extremely creative in developing a number of ways that children can be in charge of their learning. Children *want* to have a say, they *need* to have a say if they are going to grow up to be responsible people.

I had been interested in creating a more stimulating educational environment and had worked to elect responsive school board members. We had a non-traditional program approved by the time our youngest daughter entered junior high school.

At first, it was a little overwhelming since Stacy had to plan her semester's work in each of her subjects to meet Washington State guidelines, projecting what she would do and when it would be completed. She grumbled that having her teacher just give assignments was so much easier. In a very short time, she was delighted with the changes. She could adapt the assignments to her interests. The teachers were relaxed and friendly.

The arts and crafts teacher did not having sewing skills and Stacy proposed some sewing projects to meet her crafts requirements. The teacher agreed and Stacy enthusiastically started sewing. She made nine items, figuring out the patterns herself.

The following fall, she entered her projects in the local interstate fair. She won several blue ribbons and one blouse had a note pinned to it, asking if she wanted to sew for a store! We must trust that children do want to learn and respond to their interests. Stacy was in the seventh grade at that time with the freedom to learn what she was highly motivated to learn. She is an adult now and has a wonderful ability to plan and organize her work.

When children are challenged in this way, it is absolutely amazing what they can accomplish. The Nation At Risk study more than a half dozen years ago indicated the need for a radical overhaul and we are still dragging our feet. Our present school (I resist calling it educational) system was developed at the beginning of the Industrial Revolution when there was a need for people to be on time and do what they were told.

It will take a revolution to provide a system that will meet the needs of the twenty-first century. Revolutions are scary, but as responsible adults, we must welcome the change.

I think we must eliminate the words "teach" and "help" from our vocabularies. Facilitate would be a more constructive term.

It is essential that we trust our children and allow them more freedom to develop at their own spectacular rate and in their own inimitable fashion. We must develop a respect for the magnitude of their tasks and the efficiency with which children learn and create a climate for them to get on with their exciting and rewarding growth.

We Drive Our Kids Crazy Unless We Understand Discipline

"You have been a bad boy! You will have to be punished!"

"I've spanked you a dozen times for this! When are you going to stop?"

"I don't know what I am going to do with that boy! He just won't behave!"

I am sure these statements have a familiar ring to every parent. They drive our children crazy!

We must also consider how the parent who says this is feeling. What is it doing to her self-esteem? We know that a parent must have a positive sense of self if the child is to develop one. I would imagine a mother isn't feeling very successful if she is saying these kinds of things very often. It drives the parents crazy, too!

Discipline is one area that concerns all parents and, I believe, needs thoughtful consideration. We've become aware that self esteem, optimism, and trust are developing during the first few months of life. Usually it is also during those early months that the infant first encounters violence. Often it starts with a slap on the hands and verbal admonition. A recent report on violence indicated that most of us learn early that love and violence are closely allied and, as a result, the home is where much violence occurs either in the form of physical or verbal abuse. The growing public awareness of battered children, wives, and husbands indicates this.

Most of us don't associate the punishment that we impart as abusive. But how is one to draw the line between a firm spanking and abusive beating? The parent says a necessary spank. The child would probably say abuse. The way to measure successful discipline is whether the child *feels* like *cooperating*.

Small children don't willfully disobey, they are trying to discover the why and wherefore of the limits in their world. Our job as parents is to learn how to provide firm limits without undermining self-esteem. That is truly challenging!

I believe that, as parents and teachers, we need to study the meaning of discipline and its effective application.

Two meanings of discipline found in the dictionary are as follows: "Training that develops self-control and character ... Acceptance of or submission to authority and control." Which discipline do we want for our children? You can't have both.

Discipline is closely related to disciple. Our children are disciples. A disciple is one who models after their leader. The children learn by watching the adults in their environment. We are the models. "Do as I say, not as I do" won't work. Character traits, how to handle feelings, relationships with people, ways to spend time and money are learned from models. Children do reflect what they see, not what we say. If adults recognize the validity of this, they will look to themselves when they see behavior they dislike in their children. Good discipline begins with positive role models. Learning how to be that model will take a lifetime. As we *struggle* to "be" and appreciate the difficulty of change, we will take the pressure off our children and free them to model after us. What a responsibility! They will be like us!

Our youngest daughter and I were returning from a weekend at the beach in a brand new car. I backed up and scraped it on a car that had parked after we were in our car. Later, as we headed home, I said several times, "I just feel awful about what I did to our new car!" At one point, Stacy said, "Well, Mother, I think it is neat!" Shocked, I asked why. She replied, "You didn't blame anyone else." Humbly, I wondered how often I had blamed others for my mistakes. I was truly impressed with the insight of a very young person.

How we feel and act regarding discipline is a reflection of a number of factors, including how we feel about people (children) and how we were disciplined as we were growing up. Research has shown that 98% of parents participating in a survey expected their children to do what they are told. It has been demonstrated that more than 60% of adults from all walks of life were fully obedient to authority, even though they understood that the result of that obedience would hurt someone.

Parents are treating children the way they were treated, even though, while growing up, they promised themselves THEY wouldn't do that to THEIR children. Often there has been no awareness and discussion regarding long range goals and methods necessary to achieve them. Nor have we considered how each of us was punished and for what we were punished.

When parents do think of goals for children—what is wanted for them as adults—they mention qualities such as caring, creativity, independence, self-discipline, honesty, and cooperation. Usually obedience is not listed as a goal. But, too often, obedience is a primary concern of parents and teachers.

Understanding the complexities of obedience is challenging. What is obedience? How does it relate to positive discipline? Obedience is to give up your own will and live under the dominion of another. We may think we want this for our small children, but how long do we want them to obey? Whom do we want them to obey? All adults? What about the stranger who wants the child to get in his car? What about the adult (more often someone they know) who wants to be sexually abusive? Much thought must go into how to deal with obedience. We really want our children to learn to be in charge of themselves.

I think our Christian heritage has influenced our attitudes and (I am personally convinced) not in the way Jesus intended. The rod of the Bible was used to guide the sheep, not to beat them but "Spare the rod and spoil the child" interpreted to mean spanking, guides many parents. My grandmother (the wife of a Methodist minister) said that biblical admonition is no better because King Solomon said it. Look how his son Rehoboam turned out. If you are not acquainted with Rehoboam, read <u>March of Folly</u> by Barbara Tuchman, who reports he "committed act of folly that was to divide his nation and lose forever its ten northern tribes, collectively called Israel."

Another frequent quote from the Bible is Ephesians 6:1; "Children, obey your parents." I believe children had to obey their parents long before Jesus came on earth and we have not changed that goal since. I think the revolutionary concept Jesus brought to us is stated in Ephesians 6:4, "Fathers do not provoke your children to wrath!" Raising children without provoking them to anger *is* a challenge! Does that mean children can do what they want? Absolutely not!

To have order in society, we recognize the need for self-discipline, responsibility, and cooperation. Blind obedience negates the opportunity for growth. Obedience does not allow learning to battle with, thinking through, and making choices; but avoids the responsibilities that decision making entails. The opportunity to learn by independent thought and action is lost.

Then the question is: How does one discipline?

First of all, there is a need to stop thinking of children as good or bad and to *start thinking of them as learners!*

Second; we must stop thinking of discipline as punishment. *It is absolutely essential that children have limits.* How we limit and what for is what we need to think through.

I believe that parents have the responsibility of enforcing firm limits in order for children to learn appropriate behavior. We know the importance of self-esteem. Positive self-esteem is or is not reinforced in daily encounters with others in their world. It is essential that children receive more positive messages than negative ones. In order to have this happen, children must learn socially acceptable behavior.

Traditionally in our country, we have used punishment as the method for teaching. Research has demonstrated that punishment doesn't teach what we had hoped it would. It has been demonstrated that children can *master* anything we want them to learn if their cognitive level is taken into consideration and the affective climate is warm and supporting. That means they have to be ready to learn and they have to feel good about themselves while they are learning it. Parents do, indeed, have a complex and challenging task, but if we are to provide guidance for our children, it is essential that we learn how to do it. We can't afford to let our children grow up without the self-discipline required to act responsibly.

I believe our *goal must be to firmly limit children, teaching them socially acceptable behavior without violating their personhood.*

Usually we have a lot of "tapes in our own heads" regarding punishment that makes this a difficult task. Added to the complexity is that our partner has his own "tapes". It means moving away from *reacting* to their behavior and together thinking responsibly about our goals as parents. We need to learn how to gain their cooperation.

Children want to please adults, but *all* of us hate to have someone interfere with what we are doing. Our job is to *stop the inappropriate behavior immediately* (he may protest), then take the time to build a good feeling between you.

"I know you want to play in the toilet but I can't let you. Let's get some nice clean water for you to play in." Thus we stop inappropriate behavior by defining it very specifically but offering an activity that will encourage discovery and feeling good about the interaction. This may be repeated many times before it is understood and responsibility is assumed to stay out of the toilet.

"I've spanked you a dozen times? When are you going to stop?" We have frequently exclaimed in our efforts to stop repetitive behavior.

Maybe it is fortunate that children want to learn more than they want to mind. Children are learning all the time, we need to be concerned with what they are learning and how.

Identifying the specific activity of concern is important, also. Too often, we say "Don't do that" without identifying what "that" is. Our grandson gave us a beautiful example of this. Nancy would say:

"We're coming to a street, Sawyer, let me take your hand." She repeated those instructions for many street crossings.

"Me hold my hand," was Sawyer's understanding of those many directions.

"We're coming to a street, Sawyer, let's stop and look for cars. No cars are coming, we can cross the street" would have given him the information he needed to be responsible for the street. When children are still babes in arms just beginning to recognize what cars are, that instruction can start whenever one crosses the street.

To give children courage to stand up against pressure to go along with the crowd is an important long term goal of self-discipline. When parents aren't there, we want our children to have both the courage and the self-discipline to live up to the values because they *believe* that it is right.

Moral development takes place at a very early age. Because the first few years of life are critical in long range development, it is imperative that parents talk about their own values and determine the best way to pass those values on to their children so that children want to choose and be responsible for those moral values as they mature.

Violating personhood either physically or verbally is not going to achieve the self-discipline and the responsibility that is needed. I don't believe we are going to have peace in this world until we can figure out a way to raise these wee ones without violating them. Our responsibility as parents is to figure out a way to gain cooperation. An added benefit of learning how to gain cooperation is that it works with adults, too.

A mother of a toddler came to me one day with this lament. "Oh, I need help! I'm hollering at my child at least a hundred times a day, 'Get out of that dryer, get out of that refrigerator', and when he put the cat in the dryer, I had had it!" We talked about how exciting the world is to a little one and how wonderful it is to discover and explore it. If you didn't know what a dryer or refrigerator was, wouldn't you be curious?

I, then, shared this story: Back when microwave ovens were brand new, a mother brought her oven to preschool to show the children how quickly cupcakes baked. The children weren't too interested, they didn't know how long cupcakes took in a conventional oven, but the mothers were absolutely fascinated. They oh'd and ah'd while we watched it bake in a couple of minutes. Then each of us had to examine that first cupcake to see if it were, indeed, done. Then each had to taste it. I pointed out that was the way toddlers were viewing their world. Everything was fascinating to them and they had to discover all about everything. What a wonderful world to explore!

The concerned mother of the toddler came back to our next meeting eager to share. She said that every time she went to the dryer she would call her child:

"Johnny, do you want to help me put the wet clothes in the dryer?" and he would come running.

"Do you want to help me take the dry clothes out of the dryer?" She reported that he no longer was interested in the dryer. He had learned what it was for and it wasn't for cats. He still liked to help with the refrigerator. I pointed out, as I patted my round tummy, that most of us haven't outgrown our interest in what is in the refrigerator. Then she said the most important thing of all.

"Best of all for two weeks I have felt like a good mother!" Children cannot feel like "good" children if moms don't feel like "good" moms. The self-esteem of children is so closely allied to the parents that it cannot be ignored. We have to feel good about ourselves as parents. This is difficult in today's world where society tends to blame the parents for most of the ills and the parents have had very little opportunity to learn how to parent.

When parents are yelling no "a hundred times a day" they don't feel like good parents.

"No, no, you will fall!" Instead, let's give them just a little boost to help them get where they want to go. They will feel as if they did it themselves and they can survey their world from up high rather than down low. It will give them an exciting new perspective.

"No, no, don't touch!" Instead, let's show him how to touch very lightly or to look without touching, appreciating that they are learning how to treat the object.

"No, no, you'll make a mess!" Instead, show them how to do it (pour the milk) without spilling.

"No, no, you will get dirty!" Sometimes it is important to get dirty in order to learn something valuable, just as it is important to learn that sometimes it is important to stay clean. The important thing is that we need to learn how to limit without diminishing their personhood (and ours). Otherwise, children are learning they get in trouble when they learn and adults get in the way. We do not want that.

Another very important way to teach respect for limits is to evaluate the way we model respect for society's limits. A daily limit, for example, is the traffic speed limit. Do we assume responsibility to drive within the limit or do we justify breaking it? Children are incredibly young when they begin to recognize adult limits and our attitude toward them. Our children may decide to choose different social and legal limits to break.

A high school student was walking into the classroom with several girls beside him talking about the speeding ticket he had received. One young lady asked what his dad had said. He had been grounded for a month was the reply.

"Oh, how awful!" the girls exclaimed, "whatever are you going to do without the use of a car?" However, the young man said that he was with his dad the next day when his dad received a ticket and nothing more had been said about the grounding since.

The models we provide are important aspects of children learning and accepting limits.

Children want and need limits. The important adults in their environment need to assume responsibility for the setting of socially acceptable limits and enforcing them while respecting their personhood. That means firmly limiting without scolding or spanking. There is a great difference between "You are a bad boy. You need to be punished" and "I can't let you do that" (defining 'that' very specifically) let us go find something fun to do." It is an indication of caring and understanding. It is essential that these be taught in a positive way so that children grow up responsible and appreciating the value of limits rather than feeling resentment and antagonism toward limits and the people who impose them.

When we treat children with respect and dignity, we won't be driving our children crazy.

We Drive Our Kids Crazy Unless We Are Honest

"Mommie, telephone!"

"Honey, tell them I'm not home, I just don't have time to talk right now."

Children are honest! They don't know how to lie, until we teach them. Honesty is essential for healthy social and emotional development. Children are totally congruent. Their whole bodies reflect how they are feeling. We drive children crazy when we are not honest with them or others!

A roadside sign warns: "Living without trust, is like driving in the fog." Honesty is essential to trust. Trust is essential to positive relationships with people. Positive relationships are essential to a happy and productive life.

"The children get plenty of time to socialize, when will they begin to learn." This statement is often heard at preschool and reflects our naivete regarding the complexity of social development and a simplistic view of learning.

Learning is too often equated with academic achievement. Socialization seems so easy. If children can leave mother and play with other children, socialization is thought to be complete. However, successful relationships with people is a value that takes a great amount of skill, honesty, and caring. Most of us still have much to learn and our children will be like us.

Readiness for kindergarten with emphasis on the academic, too often becomes the main goal of the years before school. Our all-important aim is to provide the best possible times for the ages the children are, rather than trying to get them ready for the succeeding year. If every child lives each year to the fullest, they will be ready for the next year.

Too often, we are busy preparing preschoolers for kindergarten, kindergartners for first grade, elementary children for junior high school and high schoolers for college. We need to concentrate on appreciating and enjoying the now. Our awareness of the importance of honesty in our own social and emotional development and providing a supporting emotional climate will best prepare us and our children for the years ahead. Modeling the resolution of conflict, negotiating differences, dealing with our own anger constructively, enjoying each moment is a definite challenge and is too often left to chance.

A Sanskrit thought is worth remembering: "Yesterday is already a dream and tomorrow is only a vision but today well-lived makes every yesterday a dream of happiness and every tomorrow a vision of hope."

Emphasis on academic achievement during the preschool years may undermine the self-esteem which is vital to success in school. If children enter school with positive self-esteem, in other words, if they believe they are capable of learning—if their learning attempts have been successful in the past—if learning has been rewarding and fun—if they enjoy other children, they will enter school ready to learn the "basics" *if* they are presented at the child's readiness level. Frequently we make children fit the system rather than the system adapt to the children's needs and readiness levels.

Academic achievement is not the most important asset in achieving mature adulthood. More people are unsuccessful in their marriage and careers because they cannot get along with people, rather than their lack of knowledge or skills. A study of people in Who's Who has shown that many of them received average (or below) grades in school, (Edison, Einstein, John and Robert Kennedy and most recently, Dan Quayle are publicized examples.)

Most of the problems in today's world result from poor relationships with people. Technologically, we are zooming ahead. Our relationships with people haven't improved much since the beginning of recorded history.

Our understanding and awareness of the importance of social and emotional development and our *modeling* positive emotional and social honesty will be the best method of preparation.

Social and emotional growth begins at birth (very possibly in the womb) and is tied closely to self-esteem. Responding quickly when that brand new wee one cries is essential. Too often, some well-meaning neighbor or friend says: "Now don't run every time that baby cries, you will spoil him. He just wants to be held." We know that we need to run when babies cry, it is the only way they can tell us they need something. It won't spoil them and it is important and comforting for them to be held. After all, they have just spent nine months being held most securely very close to the heart.

When our fourth child was an infant, he had tummy troubles. By the time this wee one came along, I had learned much and loved to hold babies. I held him whenever his tummy hurt. When I quit nursing him, the tummy problems worsened. We tried many things, but nothing seemed to help. People told me I had spoiled him by holding him so much and he cried in order to be held. It worried me, but I *knew* something was hurting and continued to hold and rock him whenever he was miserable.

When he was eighteen months old, a dietician friend of mine told me about an article in her journal. Research showed that the linoleic fatty acid in corn and soy bean oils were helping some children with allergies. I checked with my doctor and he said it was a food and couldn't hurt. We tried a soup spoonful a day and almost over night, he was a different child. He was happy to play, did not need to be held, and thoroughly enjoyed the independence. I was reassured that holding a hurting child had been comforting for us both and certainly had not spoiled him.

Babies at birth are the most dependent of earth's creatures and they are dependent for a longer period of time. Dependency does not create positive feelings unless there is a great abundance of cuddling love. Babies have only one way to let us know their needs and that is through crying. If the "significant others" come immediately when babies cry, they begin to develop feelings of worth. The dependency feelings will begin to be minimized when they realize they are responded to quickly. Somebody comes when they call.

The more quickly they develop these feelings of security and worth, the less dependent they will be as they grow older. They will be free to grow into independence as they sit up, creep, walk and then move into the world outside the home. There will be no need to cling to mother.

The infants will be developing trust in the people that care for them and optimism that the world that they have come into is good.

It is a fruitful beginning of preparation for academic success many years down the road, which is such an important priority to many.

We are born with the ability to feel. We learn how to feel about those feelings. Our feelings have to be honest and congruent with our words and actions in order to socialize with integrity. Respect for our emotions, using them constructively takes honesty. Honesty has to do with truth. Life is searching for the truth. Our search has to be based on honesty with ourselves and honesty with others.

We have to learn to accept our feelings as alright, identify how we feel about our feelings, learn to match our words to our feelings (congruence) in order to model for our children the importance of honesty in our emotional and social development. We have to be congruent to build mature social relationships. And it is true that socialization begins at birth as well as how we feel about our feelings.

- "That is no way to feel,

- You mustn't feel that way,

- Your feelings are too easily hurt,

- That didn't hurt, don't cry, take it like a man."

All are statements that discount feelings, but are frequently said. They teach children to suppress their feelings, not to understand and respect their feelings. We are taught to hide our feelings with "white lies". However, if our words don't match our feelings we are lying in spite of what we say, and our body language belies the message, which is confusing.

We think learning to "socialize" is easy and accomplished early but unfortunately, this is not so. It is one of the most difficult tasks we have and one that, generally speaking, we have not learned to do well as adults.

How many of us are congruent? How many of us relate to people in honest and positive ways? How many of us recognize our anger and can express it in constructive fashion so that the relationship is enhanced rather than diminished? How many of us have easy rapport in our relationships with husbands and children, friends, and neighbors? How many of us are non-judgmental of race, creed, and color? Certainly most of the problems in today's society result more from failure in relationships than lack of knowledge or skills.

The statistics on the number of emotional problems stun us. Maybe if we took the pressure away from academic achievement and believed totally that social and emotional development were of utmost importance and made them top priorities, both for ourselves and for our children, we could develop the self-esteem that is essential to healthy growth and development, as well as academic achievement. It might move toward reducing the problems that plague society today. Certainly, the present system isn't working with children having children, the mental illness, the run-away children, and the suicide rate.

I was speaking to a group of parents regarding learning, mentioning that spanking was not a positive way to teach limits. One of the parents pointed out that she no longer was spanking her child. I said, "Good, what are you doing instead?" She replied, "I just say 'That's a stupid thing to do.'"

Children are the most incredible learners of all. Unfortunately, they learn quickly and efficiently that they are not OK with the messages we send like "That's a stupid thing to do."

To become a fully functioning person is our goal for each child. It means committing ourselves to growth into self-actualizing persons. Our children will be like us! If we work hard at assuming responsibility to understand ourselves, honesty in our relationships with people, and achieve the changes necessary for our own growth, we will take the pressure off our children. When we discover how difficult it is to change ourselves, we will modify our demands on them.

They will be free to choose our priorities, our values, our emotional stability, our social attitudes, our honesty. Too often, they resist our values in order to establish their separate sense of selves. If we encourage their freedom to develop independence, they will be unencumbered with anger and bitterness and will be free to evaluate our values without rancor. We must learn to measure our success with our children at each interaction by whether there are "stars in their eyes". We have a challenge to become models for our children, and maybe, just maybe, we won't drive our children crazy.

We Drive Our Kids Crazy
Unless We Are Joyful

The Egyptian god Osiris had a quiz for those appearing in the underworld for judgment. The crucial questions were, "Did you find joy?" and "Did you bring joy?" If a person could answer affirmatively, he was given back his "khaihit" (measure of continued existence). If not, he was taken away and eaten by a hippopotamus.

I think many of us would be eaten by the hippo. I certainly wish I had appreciated the importance of joy when our children were small. I think many of us are caught up in the stress and pressures of the day to day activities and forget that we have only one life and it is for joyful living.

Joy is an emotion we can experience every day when we learn to look for joyful moments and appreciate their presence. As I have pondered ways to help parents prevent the mistakes that I made, I think enjoyment of our families is so important. Joy, for me, is best defined by a *deep abiding gladness* which comes as a result of love.

Love is an art. Like any art, it requires long hours of study and practice in order to understand. For instance, we expect to spend long hours practising our music or athletics in order to perfect our skills (often eight or more hours a day). In order to perfect the art of loving, it is important to consciously practice love, which means we have to understand just what love is.

I John 4:8 of the Christian Bible states, "There is no fear in love but perfect love casts out fear. For fear has to do with punishment, and he who fears is not perfected in love."

We need to eliminate words like obedience, submission and punishment, which causes fear and interfere with positive relationships that reinforce self-esteem.

Our *want* is a perfect human being to love, but maybe our *need* is to develop an imperfectionist view of life in order to love without judgment and be loved. The parent wants to be a perfect parent, but think of the burden that imposes on the child. He has to be perfect, also. Too often, the message we give is that we love them *when* they behave. Let us accept our humanness and our children's humanness and love them without judgement as they joyfully discover their world.

Too often, the tragedies of the world and the pressures of parenthood have been stressed, but let us daily emphasize the *joy*, a deep abiding gladness, of living with children. It will help us toward an understanding of true love.

"One hundred years from now it will not matter what kind of house I lived in, the kind of clothes I wore, or what my bank account was. What will matter is that I was important in the life of a child." (Author unknown).

Children are born with stars in their eyes. They are thoroughly and excitedly involved in living and are living life to the hilt. They feel their emotions with their whole bodies. They show their joy from the top of their heads to the tip of their toes but they also are totally involved when they are angry. They were born with the *ability* to feel but we teach them *how* to feel about those emotions. Let us protect their right to their emotions and help them to appreciate them.

Anger is an emotion that interferes with our joy as parents. It usually makes us uncomfortable, because "good" children shouldn't get angry. Our parents were not comfortable with anger and that discomfort has been passed on to us. When our children show their temper, it makes us feel we are failing as parents, but anger is an emotion of worth if we use it to change our environment for the better. Too often, we, as parents, punish the display of anger rather than help children recognize the feeling and explore the cause of the anger and help them solve the situations so they will know how to handle anger in the future.

It is important to remember that often, constructive change has not occurred until someone was angry enough to find a way to resolve the situation in a positive way. Learning to use anger constructively is the road to emotional health. While we are painfully learning to model the constructive use of anger, let us enjoy the healthy way our children display their anger.

Our job is to learn how to love a plain human being in a joyful way instead of expecting perfection. (The Latin *amor* (love) is close to the Greek word *amusso*, which means to choke. Often overprotection is a substitute for love.) Our measurement of successes will be: "Are we achieving deep abiding gladness?"

I expect you are saying, "That sounds great on paper, but when my child is playing with an electric outlet or splashing in the toilet, how am I going to stop it?" Punishment is often the method used, and it will produce fear. Fear of the toilet or fear of the punishing parent? Why not try picking the child up in your arms and saying seriously and lovingly, "I can't let you touch that electric outlet; it will hurt you, and I love you and don't want you hurt" then find something interesting for the wee one to do. "Oh," you say, "but he'll go right back there, the first chance he has." That is true. But it is also true when you punish. How many times have you heard, "I've spanked you a dozen times for that. When are you going to stop!"

Fortunately, a child wants to learn and will continue to explore, which is necessary for growth. It is our responsibility to define behavior specifically, to limit lovingly and firmly until the child develops an understanding of the behavior expected and the self-discipline for appropriate behavior. It is a continuing growth process. Let us remember that we have a few years to accomplish this. Too often we expect instant success.

A woman wise in the ways of children told me when my oldest was small, "You know in the Bible, where it says you are to forgive seventy times seven? When you are working with children, expect to tell them seven hundred times seven before you expect them to remember. Then you will be pleased when it doesn't take that long. After more than thirty years, I still think that is excellent advice. It is important for the adults to provide firm limits, motivating cooperation until the child understands and assumes responsibility. Our job is to provide guidance so children will want to cooperate. Fear doesn't allow for *feeling* like cooperating.

Often as parents we expect children to obey and respect us as if that can be commanded; but our responsibility is to learn how to provide a climate of love so they will want to respect us. Too often, we impose on our children standards of behavior which we ourselves do not meet.

The way we relate to our children depends on our view of human nature. Do we believe that babies are born bad (born in sin?) and we have to teach them to be good? Or we may believe they are born neutral and what they become is dependent on their environment. I believe along with David in Psalm 8:5, "Yet Thou has made him (man) little less than God," that a baby is born good and that with providing a loving environment we can trust him to become a loving human being.

We are learning much about the influence of drugs and alcohol that is causing babies to be born without the ability to develop conscience. Again, we must, as responsible adults, assume responsibility to avoid pregnancy until we are ready to be responsible for that wee one growing in the womb. We have so much to learn about what can be done with those suffering babies.

Our need is to love, to find that deep abiding gladness that is joy and enhance an environment that will keep children joyful. Let us watch children as they discover their world. Much of it has become commonplace to us, and we can re-discover and appreciate it again through their eyes.

When our two year old grandson was visiting us, I discovered him with his nose pressed to the window, looking directly into the eyes of a raccoon who had his nose pressed to the window on the other side. How often I have enjoyed that mental picture of that inquisitive joy.

As we *enjoy* the world around us, we are building a positive self-esteem in our children. We are saying important things to them like, "You are fun to be with, you are important, I enjoy you," in a wonderful way.

There is much of wonder and joy in the world. Children are responsive to wonder. The wonder of the crocus peeping through the black earth, the wonder of the pink blossoms floating on the tree, the wonder of the sunset with its pinks and lavenders, riotous reds and subtle blues; the wonder of the snowcapped mountains with fleecy clouds hovering around them, the wonder of a squirrel running along a telephone wire, the wonder of the refreshing breeze caressing the face, the wonder of the softness of the pussy willow, the wonder of the waves lapping on the beach, the wonder of the feel of velvet, and...best of all...the wonder and the joy of settling down in mother's arms cuddly and warm from a bath.

Isn't the world a wonder-full place? It is important to learn that the world is good. It is the only world we have, so let us build a feeling of joy in the good things on this earth and a sense of responsibility to help change the not-so-good.

Let us search for ways to build a positive image of man and the world and its responsiveness to change. We won't drive our children crazy if we provide joy, deep abiding gladness. If we keep the stars in the eyes of children they will affirm the joys that are jewels to enjoy and treasure. Each day ask those two crucial questions: "Did I bring joy? Did I find joy?" and find delight in the answers.

We Drive Our Kids Crazy With Inadequate Child Day Care

"Do you know a good child care center? The one our child attends is so filthy dirty, my wife and I feel we need a shower after we have been there," inquired a college music teacher. He indicated that he didn't think his child would know the difference, so he was leaving him there until they found another center.

"There was an electric quality in the center, when I arrived to leave my child one morning. Uncertain, I looked around to find out what was happening. Every child was motionless and looked frightened. Then I saw a teacher spanking a child. I suddenly realized how damaging a spanking could be. After that, I just couldn't leave my child there. So I walked out, called in sick, and spent the day searching for another center for my child." Thus, a parent described the moment she began to evaluate the kind of care she wanted for her child.

Providing quality child day (or night) care needs to be a major responsibility for a community. Quality child care is too costly for most parents to pay. Alone, however, it will not ease the dilemma of the family when both parents are working outside the home. The family relationship is complex and there are no quick solutions.

With obvious pride, an avant-garde drama professor, whose office was next to mine, said he helped his wife with her housework. He was dumbfounded when he realized what a "put-down" that was. He thought he had overcome his chauvinism, but was quick to realize the difference between "helping" and "sharing". If men and women are assuming joint responsibility to earn the living, it is necessary to develop joint responsibility for home and children.

Statistics indicate that while more than half the nation's women are working outside the home, men are not sharing responsibility for doing "women's work". This is found to be true in communist countries also.

For example, most men and the companies they work for, believe the wife should stay home with a sick child.

Slowly the pattern is changing. Some families are choosing not to move at a company's request. Paternity leave and flex-time are beginning to be considered. Many European countries are more advanced in providing flex-time and child care benefits. More often than not, when flex-time is considered, it is to ease traffic and environmental concerns rather than to meet families' needs.

The old societal message of "a woman's place is in the home" is slow to die. It has a great deal to do with the guilt women feel when they go to work—even when an inflationary economy is requiring more money to provide an adequate living *and* her husband totally supports the decision to work. Guilt increases if she recognizes the importance of the early years, and quality child care is difficult to find (or more than can be afforded).

When I was director of the Parent Cooperative Program at the college, I tried to find ways to integrate the "working outside the home" parents and the parents "working inside the home". The working for pay parents didn't want to be with the working at home parents because it would intensify the guilt they felt about working. The at home parents didn't want the income-producing parents in their program, because it would make them feel guilty that they weren't working. Parents feel guilty!

Anger develops if her husband "helps" her with the work rather than "sharing" the responsibility. There is a very different message given in the husband *joins* in planning and preparing the meal, rather than setting the table—however willingly—when *asked*.

If he believes it is *her* job to stay home with sick children, or it is *her* job to find adequate child care, since *she* is going to work, the anger that is generated (and often hidden), is debilitating. If "super mom" has to put in a full work day, then come home to a "second shift", the physical work load is devastating.

Just as it is important for women to share with husbands the heavy burden of earning a living, it is necessary to remove the sexism associated with "women's work". When a mere 7-13 percent of our families fit the traditional model of father at work and mother at home with children, it is important to be creative in developing new models for child care.

The parent involvement child care model is the best solution I have found.

The Community Colleges in the State of Washington help the parents organize and operate their Parent Cooperative Preschool Centers. Parents attend an evening seminar once a month, concentrating on learning how children learn and how to cooperate with that learning. A second monthly meeting gives parents an opportunity to conduct the business of the center, with the facilitator *they* have hired, to plan the program for the children in order to have intimate awareness of the center's climate and a personal acquaintance with their children's friends and how the program is working.

When the parent cooperative preschool program was started about 1940 in Washington State, it was designed for "at home moms". It has been adapted to fit the needs of parents who are working outside the home.

Parents interview and hire the facilitator/parent educator, as well as the additional staff. Since all the parents (both moms and dads) spend some time in the center, they have a good "feel" for the relationship of the staff with the children.

"It would be pretty hard to get a porno ring going here. There are parents coming and going all the time!" As one parent said, when the sex abuse in preschool articles (the long-lasting court case in California) was often in the news.

When a number of parents with different ideas about child rearing, education, growth, and development organize a center together, a pretty sensible program evolves. The quote, "conflict leads to frustration but frustration wisely handled, leads to growth" is apt. Learning how to resolve the conflicts is an important part of the program. When some parents believe that children should be learning their "academic basics" in preschool and other parents want freedom with "no limits", it takes real skill on the part of the facilitator to guide their negotiations developing a program both can feel good about.

The seminar gives them an opportunity to explore new ideas and how to make them work. The business meeting gives them time to plan the implementation of those ideas. The staff can try the plans and all can evaluate the effectiveness.

Keeping the "stars in the children's eyes" is the best measure of effectiveness. If children are interested and involved, the plan is working. When the adults are having to tell the kids frequently to sit still, listen, don't bother your neighbor, do what you're told, the program definitely is *not* working. It is absolutely essential to measure the effectiveness of any program by the "stars in the eyes" of children. When the "stars" aren't there, it is the adults who look for ways to get the "stars" back.

The facilitator/parent educator is the clue to a successful program. This person is responsible for implementing the child care program and the happy cooperative involvement of the parents. After 20 years of working with parents and facilitators in parent cooperatives, I know that it takes very special people to work supportively with parents and their children in the same setting.

Children do behave differently when parents are there. This is often the excuse child care center staff use to keep the parents out. It is vitally important for all to learn how to relate to each other in this kind of situation, because parents are often dealing with children in front of their own parents and people in the supermarket.

When children act up in public, there are usually two reactions. If the parent picks up the child in a loving way, the unspoken message seems to be: "What that child needs is a good spanking." If the parent grabs the child in a punishing way, the unspoken message bystanders send is quite different.

"Why are you dragging that child around? Can't you see he is tired?" No matter what the parents do, they feel guilty.

It is my opinion that a parent/child/facilitator relationship is so very complex, because of the subjective relationship between parent and child. No parent wants to be told how to parent and yet every parent needs all the up-to-date information possible regarding how children learn, how to cooperate with that learning and how to strengthen and enhance family life. This is a constant challenge for the facilitator and takes incredible people skills. Fortunately, parents sense this when they are hiring. They also have the power to terminate ineffective facilitators and the staff.

With flex-time at the work place, coming in early for 30 minutes a day will allow the freedom to participate for the two hours a week, which can be scheduled to match needed time in the center. Without flex-time, parents can serve before and after work for shorter periods several times a week.

In order to provide quality care, a high adult/child ratio is necessary to give the children the attention they need. The parent involvement provides the adults needed without the need to hire additional staff with the salaries necessary. Minimum wages are often paid, which means minimum qualifications. The parents are subjectively involved and can provide the care children require.

It would be great if the center could be at the workplace. Most parents tell me that it takes one or more hours daily to drop off and pick up children from sitters. Business, industry, and government must overcome their prejudice; another barrier to overcome, is some parents' reluctance to mix their work world and their children's world.

More and more information is available regarding the advantages to the employer: improved morale, less absenteeism, more productivity, and less turnover. It is costly to train new staff.

Neighborhood elementary schools can be considered for child care space. Many schools are providing before and after school care. Some parents face the problem of finding one center for infants, another center for their older preschoolers, and a third center for after school care.

Parents who are involved in their children's program feel that it offers support and alleviates guilty and anxiety. The families become good friends, and since many young parents do not live near their own families, these friends become an extended family. Because both children and parents know each other well, they often trade "babysitting" on weekends in order to find time for that very important intimate "husband/wife" relationship.

Parent cooperative child care centers can include children with disabilities. The parents of the "normal" children discover there are real people underneath even the most disabled children. The parents of the uniquely challenged children begin to realize that maybe it is because the child is two that he behaves that way, rather than because he has a disability.

The children are great. They accept each other in a beautiful way. Deanna, who at 2 rested beside Jeffy, a child with severe challenges. One day, Jeffy was not there. When told that he had gone to the hospital to have his tonsils out, Deanna cried.

"How can I go to sleep, and who will put his pacifier in his mouth?" She needed him and just knew that he needed her.

Later, she wanted to ride in his wheelchair. Of course, she could not because he needed it. On their way to the park, a woman met them.

"What a cute child, what is the matter with him?" she asked.

"Nothing, he gets to ride and I have to walk!" was Deanna's spirited answer.

She moved away for a year. When she returned to the center, the first thing she did was to ask for Jeffy, running over to give him a kiss.

One day, she told her mother that she had dreamed Jeffy was walking. A few days later, Jeffy's mother reported that Jeffy was to get braces. Uncanny! Maybe children are psychic and we ignore or deny it.

It is the kind of program that everyone said would not work and did. One young learning-disabled child care aide was beginning to feel that his job was just "babysitting". He attended a conference for the disabled, where there was discussion of the impossibility of integrating the able-bodied and disabled children in the same child care setting. He spoke up, explaining our center to them. After answering the numerous questions, he returned believing that he was a "professional" in a very important program.

Of course, I need to add that it took a knowledgeable, sensitive, non-judging, "people" person to facilitate such a parent involvement center.

Parent cooperative child care centers can meet in the high schools. It becomes a laboratory for the high school students enrolled in child development classes, giving "hands on" experience with children. Parents do participate and the interaction between parents/children/students is very effective. High school students learn very real reasons not to get pregnant.

One of the arguments against the parent cooperative approach to child care makes no sense at all.

"Working parents just do not have time to add participation in their child's care to their already overwhelming responsibilities." I recognize the dilemma. Parents who have participated in our program found so much support and relief from guilt that they loved it. These years are too important to turn over to someone else!

Creating ways to strengthen the family must become a national priority. We need to be imaginative in developing new ways to provide support and renewal so necessary to live productively in our increasingly stressful world.

Our children are our future. What they are learning *now* regarding their values, attitudes, morals, self-discipline, and responsibilities will shape our nation when they are adults. We must quit driving our kids crazy! They will become our future. The future is NOW.

We Drive Our Kids Crazy With Religion and Without Religion

Saying the Lord's prayer is one of my early memories. When I came to the phrase, "Thy will be done on earth as it is in heaven," I earnestly added to myself, "but Lord, let me have some fun first." In retrospect, I think I associated the long hour spent in church with what God wanted me to do all the time and I didn't like sitting still.

Jesus said that we were to "become as little children if we were to inherit the Kingdom of Heaven." As a child, I was trying as hard as I could to grow up and that statement was a puzzle to me.

When I was a little older, I was disturbed by "Forgive us, as we forgive," because I knew that deep down inside, no matter how hard I tried, I wasn't very good at forgiving. It seemed as if we were to *earn* our forgiveness by God. That seemed a contradiction, since we did not have to *earn* God's Grace. I struggled with that for many years.

After enrolling at Whitworth College for my freshman year about fifty years ago, my father asked me what courses I had signed up to take. I listed them, ending with Bible, which was required for all freshmen. He then asked what part of the Bible and I replied that it was the first five books of the Old Testament. My father, who went to church every Sunday, was the son of a minister, said blessings at meals, totally surprised me by exclaiming in dismay, "What business do they have spending that much time on the Old Testament. If they are going to study the Bible it should be the first four books of the New Testament. Well, learn it long enough to pass the tests, then forget it!"

Wow! During the course, I pondered that outburst but when we were told to skip the chapter on Lot sleeping with his daughters (I am sure it is the only chapter everyone in the class read) I began to have some beginning understanding. I think that concern led to much of the questioning that was involved in my development and understanding of religion.

I also tried to understand what God was going to do about Gandhi, whom my very spiritual mother admired so much. He was not a Christian yet I thought only Christians were going to heaven. What was God going to do about him? If *he* couldn't get in heaven, I didn't think God was a very loving Heavenly Father.

When I married, I understood that I was to be submissive to my husband and when our life was not going too well, I studied the Bible and tried hard to follow Paul's teaching. Billy Graham had a regular column in the paper I read at that time and he reiterated Paul's teaching. I tried hard! I wondered why I had so many questions when I was trying so hard to be "religious". Later, I learned that Billy Graham was about my age so he was a very young man when he was writing that column.

I pondered often the submissiveness that was so often preached. Certainly there was an expectation that women were to be submissive. I didn't question that so much but the Bible said slaves should obey their masters. Did that mean Jesus approved of slavery? Of course, the masters were to treat their slaves well as were the husbands their wives. The struggle to understand submission was filled with so many questions.

Later, much later, I discovered Leslie Weatherhead and Paul Tournier and felt I had come home! What a tremendously liberating force these two great men were in my life. Weatherhead was a Methodist minister as was my grandfather. He was "an angry old man and I feel I must get the fire out of my bones", as John Wesley would say, "before I die", after a lifetime in the ministry. He was expressing the same questions and concerns that I had. I was so relieved that such a well-known Christian minister had the same questions.

Tournier was a Christian psychiatrist. He helped me to understand forgiveness and grace. Indeed, one does not *earn* God's grace. His books became a guiding light in my spiritual growth. I also learned that submissiveness was the Roman rule for both women and slaves about which the budding Christian faith could do nothing. The revolutionary message that Christ brought was that husbands and masters were to treat their wives and slaves with respect. It was in the sixth century that the church decided (by one vote) that women were more than animals.

I struggled with the meaning of "love thy neighbor as thyself." I thought it was selfish to love yourself. Through the years, as I grew spiritually, I came to understand that I could not love others *unless* I loved myself.

There is so much to learn about how we grow spiritually and how to guide our children.

We drive our kids crazy with religion and we drive our kids crazy without religion. I don't think we understand spiritual growth, which is the goal of religion. Too often we work so hard at *teaching* the "fruits of the spirit" not realizing that we must *live* them.

"If man is made in God's image, how come we think God is good?" was the astonishing perceptive question my very young fourth child asked me one day.

I'll admit to shock! What kind of message was I giving him? Was it just me, or all his significant adult models? I had no answer, but I have pondered the meaning of that question forever. We *are* the models for our children.

We all know families who enrolled their children in the cradle roll at church and took them to Sunday School, church and youth groups all through their growing up years. Sometimes at least one of their children grew up to be atheists. Other families claimed atheism or at least professed no interest in religion; and often, at least one of their children grew up to be a very strict fundamentalist Christian. Religion is just one more place we drive children crazy.

God is Love. I think our comprehension of love is like dipping a teacup into the ocean and declaring that the seawater thus contained is like the ocean, ignoring the power, magnificence, beauty, and vastness! Our understanding of the power of love can be compared to ocean water in a teacup.

Teilhard de Chardin has my favorite quote regarding love. "Someday, after we have mastered the winds, the waves, the tides, and gravity, we shall harness for God the energies of love. Then for the second time in the history of the world, man will have discovered 'fire'."

We can appreciate that all transactions in our relationships with people are gifts of love or reactions to its absence. We can measure our interactions by whether those involved feel more or less loving, if we want our children to grow up sane.

Jesus said we must become as little children in order to inherit the kingdom of heaven.

As I mentioned, when I was a child and anxious to grow up, I wondered about this admonition. The longer I was involved with families, the more meaningful those words became.

We are so caught up in trying to shape our children, we forget that we are their models. They will be like us!

When our oldest children were small, I was going to be the best possible mother, but I concentrated on *their* behavior. As we had more children and more experience, I realized that if I were to be a good mother I had better concentrate on *me*. *I* had to learn ways to gain their cooperation rather than concentrating on making them "mind". I had to quit expecting them to *obey* me and learn how to "provoke not my children to wrath." *I* had to handle my anger constructively if I wanted them to handle their anger in positive ways. I had to learn how to express my feelings and listen to expression of their feelings with compassion, patience, and respect, if I wanted them to learn to identify their feelings and communicate to me how they were feeling.

Our last child was seventeen years younger than our oldest. It was the greatest learning period for me. By the time Stacy arrived I was working hard learning to thoughtfully *act* rather than react.

One night I returned from a parent meeting much later than expected and Stacy scolded as I came in. "Mother, where have you been?" My first reaction was anger and I almost answered her with, "What business is it of yours?" but fortunately, with great effort, stopped in time and said, "I'm sorry I am late, what did you need me for?" She replied, "Oh, Mom, I have to have these shorts finished to wear for cheerleading tomorrow and I can't get them right." So I helped her. Several moments later, she said contritely, "Mother, I am sorry I was cross." How happy I was that I *had* thoughtfully acted. It helped me appreciate how responsive children can be when we treat them like we would like to be treated, which, after all, *is* the Golden Rule.

It is difficult for parents to think the Golden Rule is for children. One evening I was talking to a church's couples club. I asked them how many believed in the Golden Rule? There were nods and smiles and every hand was raised.

"How many of you practice it with your children? " was my next question. There were looks of confusion among them. Then one man asked, "Which golden rule do you mean?"

"What is your golden rule?" I inquired.

"Do unto others as you would have them do unto you," several replied.

"Yes, that is mine, too." I smiled in agreement. "Do you practice it with your children?"

"How can you and be a parent?" a puzzled dad asked.

We spent the evening discussing how parents could practice the Golden Rule with their children. After the meeting, the chairperson was confronted by one of the fathers.

"That speaker doesn't look a bit like she talks!" he exclaimed.

When the baffled chairperson asked him why, he replied, "Why, she looks so conservative."

It really is easiest to practice with children because they are so responsive.

Inspite of a long term goal of treating others like I would like to be treated, I still failed often. As I realized how hard it was for me to change *me*, the more tolerant I was of the time it took our younger children to grow and mature. It helped me to accept *our* humanness and gain an appreciation of what our children could teach me.

I have been totally dumbfounded at their insights and evaluation of adult behavior. Painful moments have come as the result of their innocent but perceptive remarks. Our oldest daughter was particularly able to share her awareness of the "put downs" of adults in their interactions with each other and caused me to evaluate myself and my interactions. Often I am completely unable to respond positively to an aggressive "put down" no matter how much intellectually I want to, I respond emotionally.

After a visit to our friends, we were gossiping critically of them. Nancy commented non-judgementally, "I *like* them and I had a good time!" I was startled and I thought why I had a *good* time too and I *like* our friends. I thought about it all the way home wondering why I was agreeing with my husband. I realized that I often had agreed with him outwardly when I really didn't inwardly. It was the beginning of examining submission, passive agreement, losing my authenticity as a person.

Much later, this oldest daughter was going to Japan for a year as an exchange student. She was looking very serious as we waited for her to board the ship. Kathy, her younger sister, searched for some comforting words. "Just think, Nancy, for a whole year you won't have to get Daddy a cup of coffee!" Submission wasn't building positive family relationships.

Our children taught me so much about judging, loving, awareness, of people and relationships. We must "become as little children" gained meaning and I was discovering how many ways I must become more like my children.

Children have a sense of wonder, an appreciation for our earth and the wonders of this world. It is so exciting for them to discover it. It *is* a beautiful earth. Let us enjoy it *with* them. How easy it is to discourage wonder; "You'll get all dirty," or, "Hurry up, we don't have time to look."Let us slow down and appreciate with our children the grandeur, beauty, and harmony of our earth. Maybe our children will grow up to appreciate and protect it rather than vandalize it.

Children are in tune with their bodies, and we teach them to ignore their instinctive awareness of their needs when *we* decide how much they should eat, when they should sleep, or when we give them food when they are tired, bored, noisy, or hurt. "Do you want a cookie to make it feel better?"

Children are honest, much to our embarrassment sometimes. Because we don't understand the growth process, we often interpret their burgeoning imaginings to be lies, when, in reality, they are as yet unable to discern the difference between reality and imagination. We may have taught them to be afraid of us, because of our punishing reactions to their developing social behavior. We can accept their "tall tales" and cooperate with their creative imaginations, helping them to learn the difference between what is real and what is imaginative. If *we* model total honesty and treat them with respect, we can help them preserve their sense of honesty.

I am afraid we adults have lost an appreciation of the importance of honesty, both at the personal and the national level. Imagination is a wonderful asset we often lose as adults but is the basis for creativity.

Children are eager to learn and learn more during their early years than we know how to teach them later on. Never again in their lifetime will they learn as much as they do during these incredibly important childhood years.

Children are loving. Their love is unconditional. How often we put conditions on our love for them. "I won't like you if you do that" is a message often sent even if we never say those words. Children are forgiving. If I say, "I'm sorry," to a child, he'll return it with a tight hug and, "I'm sorry, too, Mommie (or Daddy)" It's only an adult (our partner?) who might react with a, "Well, you should be!"As adults we are embarrassed and haven't learned to accept apologies gracefully and gratefully.

Children are fair. We may call it "sibling rivalry." In reality, our children are loudly letting us know we have some problems in our relationship with them that we need to examine thoughtfully, appreciating their awareness of what is fair. Often we put too much responsibility on the eldest. The youngest learns to manipulate both the older child and the parent and it is not fair.

Children are sensitive to feelings. This, to me, is the most amazing quality of all. A psychiatrist friend of mine told me that children are truly sensitive to people and the messages they send and we have trained it out of them by the time they reach 12-14 years of age.

Once I commented to our 14 year-old son on his sensitivity to the people around him and he replied that he used to be but wasn't nearly as aware as he once had been. It was fascinating to me that he recognized the change. People spend many years learning to be psychiatrists and counselors trying to develop sensitivity to people's feelings but never do regain that early awareness. Let us appreciate the sensitivity of children and free them to grow with it rather than to stifle it.

"Train up a child in the way he should go" has been an erroneous guiding principle. We train animals. I like a more accurate translation I read: "Educate a child in the way *that is his own*". I believe that is an inspiring goal. We have to learn *their* way, not impose our way.

Let's learn to "become as little children!"

Let us assume the reponsibility to become childlike and work at understanding the importance of love as an infinitely capable creative force and we will no longer drive out children crazy.

Our goal can be to model an inspiring *faith* to live by, a comfortable *self* to live with, and to know the *purpose* for which we live. Our children will be like us!

"Truly I say to you, unless you turn and become like children you will never enter the kingdom of heaven." (Matthew 18:3)

We Drive Our Kids Crazy When We Tell Them They Can Do It If They Try

"Just try a little harder," or "You can do it if you try" are phrases often heard. Parents tell it to children, teachers to students, husbands to wives, wives to husbands, employers to employees, and parent educators to parents.

What does the phrase imply? You aren't trying! You could do it if you tried. I believe children are doing the best they are able. I believe that parents are doing the best they are able. I believe that we are all doing the best that we can. If we had more knowledge and understanding we might do things differently, but I don't believe we would be able to work any harder at it. Unless we had met with so many failures that we have given up and that admonition wouldn't help in those cases either.

When working with court-referred abusive parents I have found that they were doing the best they were able to do. They were treating their children as they had been treated. They knew no other way. I found many of them responsive and relieved when they learned there were different ways to parent. It wasn't easy to change (no change is easy) and it took awhile.

One young couple were referred to me because their infant had been abused and was failing to thrive. I learned that the father spanked the wee one because it hurt him too much to hear it cry. A friend had told him that he started spanking his baby at three weeks when it cried and it never cried anymore. This dad, with a very tragic early life, appreciated the difference between his childhood and what I was recommending.

"Just think how different I might have been if I had been treated like that!" was his insightful remark.

Late one night when circumstances became overwhelming, he called me to say, "Why does everyone else have a good family life but me!"

It has been my experience that children try hardest of all. They do want to please us. In fact, they are so dependent on us for everything that they feel deeply the need to please us. They are doing the best they are able for the developmental level they have reached. They behave the way they do because they *need* to. It is only when they have done their best for a long period of time and it is *not* appreciated, that they give up and withdraw or act out against the system. We are driving them crazy!

It is important to keep our expectations within their reach. Often we demand of children behavior we have not achieved ourselves. For example: "That is no way to behave! If you would just try, you could control your temper! Now go to your room and when you are nice you can come out." The child is learning to hide feelings. He is not learning to deal with anger constructively.

Most of us do not handle anger well. We would be absolutely furious if we were sent to our room when we are angry. (Just imagine your spouse saying it to you.) Using anger constructively has not been a learning objective. As we learn to recognize the feeling of anger, (how many of us have shouted, "I'm not angry!" in vehement tones) analyze the cause of our anger, and then examine how to resolve the situation so we don't have to get angry about that issue again, we can become models for our children.

Until then, let us learn to respond more empathetically to our children. As one parent said during a group discussion of anger, that she was just discovering that she wasn't handling her anger too well. She realized that she had been angry every morning for eight years as she tried to get her husband to put his clothes in the laundry instead of leaving them on the floor.

As we recognize the difficulty of handling our anger more constructively, we will appreciate the children's honesty in handling their anger. They display it from the top of their head to their tippy toes, a healthy way to get it out of their system. However, we, as parents, are most anxious and impatient, feeling intense guilt when our children display anger. After all, we were taught not to show anger. When our children engage in a temper tantrum, we feel we are failing as parents. They aren't supposed to do that!

"If you would just try, you wouldn't wet your pants!" It is important to believe that the child wanted to get there in time (if he is old enough to recognize the feeling and to know what to do about it). It is pretty difficult for a small child to gauge these things and it is easy not to allow enough time to get where he needs to go.

One father told me he would have expected his child to get to the bathroom in time except he just happened to be looking out the window and saw his son leave the group of children and run recklessly to the house. Then he saw him stop suddenly and sprattle his legs, standing still with an intense look on his face. The father knew exactly what was happening and he knew that he had tried. He could thank him for trying and help him to feel alright about the failure.

"If you just try, you could get better grades!"

That is assuming the child is not trying to get a good report card. Getting good grades in school has been made very important. A more accurate assumption could be that he has done his best and is disappointed both with the report and your reaction. It is pretty disillusioning to have done your best and still fail to meet teacher and parental expectations. Instead of blaming the child, maybe we had better critically examine a system that makes six year old children feel like failures.

Children who are doing their best and fail to meet societal expectations will find their self-esteem damaged unless the mistakes are viewed as stepping stones to success. When children try and are labeled failures, they will soon quit trying or act out in anger against the system. After spending 180 days in the slow-reading group, children lose self-esteem and often quit trying. Our remedial programs are not very successful at overcoming that damage.

We drive children crazy when we tell them they can do it if they try.

It is important to eliminate the phrase and attitude "you can do it if you try" from our language and substitute an approach that will appreciate the effort and reinforce positive feelings toward the learning and provide an environment where mistakes are viewed as stepping stones or challenges to achievement.

An honest realization that the child is doing his best and an appreciation for that "best" will develop the positive self-esteem, essential for continued effort and eventual success.

We Drive Our Kids Crazy When We Discount Children's Fears

"Mommie, come here quick! There is something in my room! I'm afraid!"

Eda Le Shan, my favorite family life educator and author, has told this story of her small daughter's fear of the dark. In spite of years of working as a nursery school psychologist, when her own little girl called her to her room to with this fear of the dark, Eda Le Shan "reacted" as most mothers do. "There is nothing to be afraid of in here."

"There may not be in your dark, but there is in mine!" Wendy retorted. Perception is reality.

Fears are defined as "no understanding for." To understand children's fears means to be aware of what children don't understand. Imagine the shadow of a tree blown by the wind in the moonlight and reflected on a bedroom wall. If you didn't understand shadows, wouldn't *you* be nervous?

Watch children lined up to see Santa at Christmas time. Many cling to their mothers who are eager for pictures and are expecting them to sit on this strange looking man's lap. If you didn't understand about Christmas and Santa Claus and were tiny and vulnerable, might you be afraid?

The other night we were waiting for a fireworks display. Children were playing around their parents. When the first explosion occurred, some of the smaller children screamed in fright and ran to their parents. One dad turned angrily to his shrieking son yelling, "Stop that! Right now. That is no way to behave!" He grabbed the child and dragged him after him.

Understanding fears and how they develop is an essential part of understanding children and responding with empathy to their needs.

I read a study of fears of animals: A new puppy under five weeks has no fear of humans. At seven weeks it takes two days to get acquainted; at 14 weeks it takes prolonged treatment and is always somewhat fearful. Monkeys at six to seven weeks had a slight fear of humans; at three months there is extreme distrust, and it takes a month before it will play actively; at 16 months it will crouch and rock and it will take two to three years to accept humans. If this is happening to animals, we need to be much more aware of how our infants a feeling and respond with positive support.

There is much to understand about fetal life, the birthing process, and the first few years of life and how we are driving children crazy with fears.

When we look at all the things in our world children can't understand, it explains a lot about children's fears. The *outside* world is full of strange things like the noisy vacuum cleaner, toilet (can he be flushed away? since he also has no concept of size) or a disappearing mommy who has just gone into a another room.

We can be careful about "just dropping our children off at the child care center" whether it be a church, bowling alley, or all day care. Small children are just developing time concepts and they need to learn that the parent will return. When we plan to leave a child, we need to allow an introductory time to let the child learn that the parent will return. Leave them with the promise that you will be back very soon and then return after a very short time so the child will learn that mom is coming back. Gradually, the time can be lengthened.

When a child doesn't cry when left, it may mean that he is too scared to cry! One caregiver told a mom that her child had been just fine, he hadn't moved since she had left him! Can you imagine the fear that froze him?

The *inner world* is also frightening. One can't see, smell, taste, or hear it, yet it is definitely there. It takes quite a while to sort out what's real, imagined, or dreamed. How do you explain a dream to a small child? Too often, we discount the dream or the imagined event rather than listen to what the child may be understanding regarding the world. We will also be discounting the importance of dreams and the imagination. It is vital to learn of what small children are aware. We know they can read adults with precision. There is suspicion that children may have psychic sensitivity that needs to be reinforced rather than discounted. We truly need to listen to children.

I am sure you know about *contagious* fears. We need to identify and deal with our own fears. Thunder and lightning, water, heights, dogs, spiders are some of the adult fears that often are passed on to children. I hope none of us *threaten* our children with boogie men, police, ghosts, etc. But can we be sure our children have not been threatened by babysitters or others?

Let me quote from a letter I received from a parent: "It started as a game when Scotty was two. I would hide while my husband would help him find me. The old hide-and-go-seek game, we played it before bedtime. Then we complicated the game by hiding in a dark room and yelling 'boo' when he came close. We should have recognized the first sign that we were going too far when Scotty insisted that his dad come with him. But we thought it was fun when our son got scared and ran back to his dad.

"Then one night after we tucked him in, he didn't want to go to bed because "Mr. Boo" would get him. I didn't take him too seriously and just told him to go to bed. My husband came to investigate the fussing and listened patiently. He told Scotty that he would watch for Mr. Boo and kick him out if he tried to bother Scotty. That got him through many rough nights to come.

"Needless to say, we caught on to how Mr. Boo had originated. Thereafter, we had many long talks about the scary Mr. Boo, how he was really pretend, or if we ignored him he would bother someone else." (Which is a contradictory message).

"When Scotty turned three, we made a big deal of Mr. Boo leaving and finding someone else. But he would still pop back into existence.

When we moved to the country, we again announced Mr. Boo would stay in the city and find someone else to bother. But it wasn't long before Mr. Boo found us.

As we were taking a walk a few nights ago, Mr. Boo came into our conversation. Scotty asked me why Mr. Boo liked to scare people. I reminded him that he was pretend and maybe Mr. Boo would like to be his friend because he needed someone to play with. I wonder when Mr. Boo will leave us in peace. Scotty will turn five this year.

Please tell other parents not to scare impressive two year olds—as we did. Scotty is a happy intelligent boy. I'm sorry, though, this innocent, (or should I say thoughtless?) game left its mark for such a long time."

They created a reality for Mr. Boo. Need I say more?

When our youngest was small, we were visiting cousins. Her uncle brought in a bat in a glass jar to show the children.

Stacy said: "There's no such things as bats." We explained that this was a bat. More emphatically, Stacy stated, "There's no such things as bats!" We reiterated, that, indeed, this is a bat. Almost hysterically, Stacy exclaimed, "There's no such things as bats!!" When we explained as gently as possible that bats flew at night and we usually didn't see them, Stacy then asked, "Are there witches, too?"

I would guess that ninety per cent of what children are learning, we don't know we are teaching and ninety per cent of what we *think* we are teaching, we would be shocked if we knew what our children are learning. Their perception is their reality.

We need to be very sensitive to children's fears and listen to what they are telling us about what they are learning.

There are two *major fears* not often recognized that influence us all of our lives—the fear of abandonment and the fear of engulfment. At birth, abandonment is begun by isolating the infant in the hospital nursery instead of bonding on the mother's breast. Fortunately, that is changing. However, enrolling infants in child care situations is a newly developing area for concern.

During the early years there is total dependence on parents. The fear of separation from such important people influences behavior greatly. As autonomy or separate sense of self is developing, inner conflict results. There is the need for personhood that begins to develop before the age of two and the fear of engulfment causes the "terrific two's" and their frequent "no's. They want to "do it myself" and a moment later: "Mommy, you do it." Conflict is developing between the need for independence and the fear of separation.

That conflict continues to develop, becoming acute during the teenage years. Parents are often confused by dramatic switches from the demand for independence and the reversal to dependence. Understanding those fears can do much to establish empathy for the conflict in teenagers.

As adults, marriage can become a battleground for dealing with these two unresolved fears—separation and engulfment.

I am reminded of an anonymous lyric from my youth.....

> Hold love too tightly and it will die,
>
> Hold love too lightly and it will fly.
>
> Tightly lightly, how do I know?
>
> Whether I am killing my love
>
> Or letting it go?

Your two-year-old, ten-year-old, and every other child, including the *child in each of us*, is struggling with those two fears. They influence the way we react with the significant others in our lives, influencing our relationships. Understanding this can help us resolve our own conflicts.

We can accept the normalcy of fears; don't shame or make fun of, but show the child that fear is legitimate.

Respect for children's fear is essential. Helping them understand those fears may help to eliminate them. If we can listen and learn what is causing the fears and show them the cause, those fears can be reduced, but more importantly, they will learn how to deal constructively with fears in the future.

We can find ways to trust them so they develop autonomy—the sense of their own personhood and have the courage to develop independence. It will help us understand their conflicts they are experiencing as we identify our own separation and engulfment fears.

The years before school are tender, and the learnings affect the rest of our lives. Those early days and years are "the first days of the rest of their lives!" We don't want to limit that future with unnecessary fears. Let's respect their importance so that we do *not* drive our children crazy with fears and can keep the "stars in their eyes."

We Drive Our Kids Crazy Unless We Respect Children and Their Property

Four year old Hope and her family went out to eat. As most four year olds do, she ordered a hamburger. As most four year olds are, she was slow at eating because of her intense interest in all that goes on wherever there are people. Her father helped himself to the other half of her 'burgher. Hope looked at him thoughtfully and said, "When I grow up, you'll ask me if you can have it, won't you?"

One of the underlying qualities of socially acceptable behavior is concern and respect for people. Our goal is to firmly limit children, teaching them socially acceptable behavior without violating their personhood. Usually we have a lot of "tapes in our heads" regarding punishment that make this a difficult task. Added to the complexity is that our partners have their own "tapes". It means moving away from *reacting* to their behavior and thinking responsibly about how to thoughtfully *act* so our children will want to cooperate.

Respect for children is essential. If that respect for children is there, they will also respect people which leads to respect for property. While the child is learning this respect, the parents will have to limit children's behavior in such a way that they will want to cooperate and begin to assume responsibility for their actions. A large measure of a child's self-esteem is determined by society "out there," by the messages that are sent in reaction to the child's behavior.

Both parents and children are very sensitive to these kinds of messages and if children don't learn appropriate social behavior, many of these public messages will be negative and so influence their images of themselves.

We are giving children messages all the time.

If a child is at Aunt Suzie's and is allowed to explore the home, getting into everything (such as drawers,) the child will not learn to respect another's property. More importantly, the child (and the parent) will probably receive some mighty negative, usually unspoken, messages from the owner. It is unfortunate, but true, that often the hostess will allow behavior in her home that is intensely upsetting rather than to state firmly, "I can't let you play with that, but here are some things that you may play with." The irritated feelings cannot be hidden, however, and children receive and internalize the negative messages without understanding them.

The parents have a responsibility to stop behavior immediately in a firm but friendly manner whenever it does not show respect for people and property. We can explain before any activity what the acceptable behavior will be and what they can and cannot do while involved. For example, if we are going to the supermarket, we can explain to our children what they may or may not touch. We can tell them the items needed and encourage them to help find the items on the shelves and (when reachable) let them put them in the basket. Imagine how it looks to small children when we tell them they can't have anything, but we are choosing a number of items for ourselves. (Perception is reality.)

The more we can help them anticipate appropriate behavior and involve them in the process, the more it will contribute to cooperation on their part.

The way a child learns respect for adults is to show respect for him and his property. Too often, we expect children to respect the adult's property without respecting theirs. We expect them to share toys before they are old enough to understand the concept of sharing. Children have to be old enough to understand ownership before they can understand the concept of sharing. Adults make choices of what they will share. Often, we don't give children the right to make those decisions. We expect them to share a brand new trike with other children but we do not share our brand new car (sometimes, not even with our partners).

When children are small and are just beginning to learn about ownership but before they understand that when they share, the toys will be returned, it is wise to have some "non-owned" toys for sharing that are brought out when other children are there to play. To help them understand about ownership and sharing, we can ask children before friends arrive which toys they want to share and what toys should be put away while the friends are there. This will encourage an understanding between ownership and sharing.

Another method of teaching respect for property is to respect their property. Too often, toys are dumped into a toybox when children are finished playing with them. When a child wants a toy, it is difficult to find in that confusion. Many toys are tossed out in order to find the particular toy for which they are looking. No wonder their rooms are often a mess.

If many long shelves (even just boards on bricks) are furnished and toys are always put on shelves visible for choices, the child will learn better habits as well as respect and care for property. Can you imagine all your kitchen utensils dumped in one big box and the frustration of trying to find the silverware?

Attitudes toward people and property are learned very early and we are modeling them all the time. So much is learned during the first few years of life. It is important to provide an environment where good habits regarding the children's belongings are developing.

Another part of teaching respect for people and property includes respect for our world. It is vital to model and help children learn to be responsible for disposal of trash right down to the tiny gum wrapper. As the signs on the wilderness trails warn: "Pack it in, pack it out." Our society spends millions of dollars each year picking up the trash that people leave. They will be paying taxes one of these years to finance that kind of clean-up, as we are paying those taxes now.

Containers in the child's room and the car will be ways we can help children learn respect for the land we live in. The vandalism that is rampant today is another indication of a lack of respect for people and property. I believe it is the result of a lack of respect for our children and of not providing an environment of respect for their individual growth and development. We are expecting behavior that is not appropriate for their ages and development. Because they are so small and vulnerable, they can only be on the receiving end. They do develop an anger and frustration at their vulnerability that may come out as destructiveness when they are older.

The vandalism is one of the visible signs that we drive kids crazy. If we are to eliminate the vandalism and graffiti that is destroying property and desecrating our countryside, we are going to have to treat our children with the respect they deserve, learn how and when they grow and develop, and do it without violating their personhood.

It means changing our thinking from scolding and spanking to "this is something I haven't successfully taught. I have to find the best way to teach it so that they will want to cooperate and assume responsibility for the appropriate behavior." They will learn to respect people and property when we respect them and their property. We will no longer be driving our children crazy and it will be visible when the graffiti, arson, and vandalism disappear.

We Drive Our Kids Crazy Unless They Believe They Can Make a Difference

Recently, our college forum was revising the mission statement for our community college. Although all students and faculty were invited, only a few students and faculty had attended. When the student body president was asked why the students had not become involved, his reply reflected a discouraging problem in our society. He said the students didn't believe their involvement would make any difference. I suspect that is why the teachers didn't come.

Only a small proportion of the citizens of this country register and vote. People don't believe it will make a difference. Yet many important decisions have been made with a very small majority. Recently, a school levy lost by nine votes. There have been times when an issue has been won or lost by one vote.

There are people who believe they can make a difference in their world...and there are people who believe the world happens to them and there isn't anything they can do about it. These attitudes are closely allied to their self-esteem and, we know, that self-esteem begins at birth. I think we want and need people who believe they can make a difference in their world.

Infants begin to learn this at birth. It is essential for wee ones to know they can make a difference in their world. The infant who cries needs to *know* that someone will come. "If I cry and someone comes, I can make a difference in my world."

The toddler who is defining the sense of self needs to *know* that "if I can make a choice (even a bad one) and something happens, I can make a difference in my world."

The preschooler who is full of questions needs to *know* that "if I talk and someone listens, I can make a difference in my world."

Too often the child chooses and the parent doesn't respect the child's choice: "Clean up your plate"..."I'm not hungry"..."Clean it up and you can get down from the table." They learn to do what the parent says instead of listening to their bodies. It may be the beginning of obesity. They also are learning they cannot make a difference in their world.

As parents, it is important to learn how to provide our children with opportunities to make choices within their age limits. It means respecting their right to make bad choices and live with the results. Giving them a choice and then discounting that choice relays the message that they cannot make a difference. (Giving them an allowance and not telling them how to spend it...but not giving them more money if they make a bad choice) will help them learn to evaluate their choices and they do make a difference.

All their lives, they are going to have to make choices that will have lasting impacts on their lives. Learning how to make wise choices is a necessary ingredient to successful living and the first fifteen years is the period when they must learn how to evaluate issues and make wise decisions. Eventually they will have to make major decisions regarding careers and marriages that will influence them their entire lives.

It is necessary to examine our methods for teaching responsible choice-making. Good choices come from having the freedom to make bad choices. What kind of choices can two's, three's, four's make?

Very small children can make choices at meals. If children are allowed to choose the food from what is offered at the table and given *tiny* amounts so they won't be overwhelmed, they are learning to respect their bodies' needs and also that adults respect them. Certainly, their tastebuds are more sensitive to strong tasting foods. There is some indication that children don't like the foods that may cause an allergic reaction. There is more wisdom in their wee bodies than we realize and we can trust them to make wise choices. It is important to avoid offering rich desserts and foods with lots of fat, salt, and sugar.

It is important that choices are made within a framework of firm limits. Complete permissiveness often results in a lack of respect for others as well as self.

Mealtime is necessary for family unity and the "meal getter's" self-esteem, so the child should be there (there is no need to become a short-order cook) but it is essential that the child can choose what and how much to eat from what is served. We have thought that children should eat what is put before them. Dad reminds them that he eats everything, not realizing that often mom doesn't cook what he doesn't like.

Bedtime is a limit for preschoolers...when to go to sleep is their choice. It is pretty hard to *make* a child go to sleep. Parents as well as children need firm limits for their children's bedtime. Dad and mom need that valuable time as husband and wife. The child can choose quiet activities (listening to records, looking at books, coloring) within their rooms until their bodies tell them it is time for sleep.

If mom and dad choose some individual quiet time while children have this quiet time in their rooms, it will make the transition easier. It is much easier to be alone when everyone else is alone too. Later, they can join together for some intimate sharing time as husband and wife, which is important.

We want respect for family which means participating in family rituals (like mealtime) but respect for each member by allowing choices within that framework.

Learning to distinguish between opportunities for choices in order to make differences and necessary limits is the parent's responsibility. Examine the number of choices your children have. How often are we limiting the choices our children can make? How often are we directing activities unnecessarily? Are *we* making responsible choices? Are we modeling appropriate discussion, weighing pros and cons, sharing decisions?

It is essential to build confidence in our ability to make choices we can live with. It is very difficult and damaging to the relationship if one partner is forced to carry the burden of decision-making because their partner never learned or lacks the confidence to make choices and assume responsibility for the decisions. If one doesn't participate in the decision-making, it is easy to blame the spouse if it isn't a wise choice.

If we are not to drive our kids crazy, it is essential we provide an environment where they can make choices and have the responsibility for those choices. Our children are growing to adulthood and need to have had the experience to make mature wise choices in choosing careers, marriage partners, political representatives, and, most important of all, becoming successful parents so they don't drive *their* children crazy.

We Drive Our Kids Crazy With Our Addictions

We are a family of readers! My husband grew up reading, as did I. It continues to be one of our favorite activities. Because we were readers, of course, it was important for our children, when they were small, to be readers and I fostered that in every way I could. After all, one "had" to be a good reader to succeed in school and later in life! When the children outgrew their naps, we progressed to a reading/rest time after lunch. As a former teacher, I knew that regression occurred in the summer so we read often during the vacation time. We developed good readers.

One weekend our adult son came home for a visit. He was in his bedroom reading, my husband was absorbed in his reading and I was sitting with a book on my lap, wishing Chip was not engrossed in his book and wondering if I should interrupt his reading in order to have a longed for visit with him. Suddenly, he came from his room and announced he was going to visit a friend. I could understand that he would want to see his friend while he was here but was disappointed that I was not going to have a chance to catch up on what was happening in his life, since he was not staying long.

As I pondered the very strong feelings I had that weekend, I thought about how isolating reading is. We did not particularly enjoy TV, but at least it was sharing more than each of us reading to our individual interests. I wondered how often we had innocently neglected building solid communication skills by isolating ourselves with books.

The next week I had to be in Seattle for the college and called Chip to meet him for supper before catching the plane home. I told him how I had felt and he admitted the same feelings that I had shared but he hadn't wanted to interrupt our reading! We had jokingly called ourselves "bookaholics" but now I was realizing that it might be a serious malady.

Alcohol and illegal drugs are generally considered addictions. One can become addicted to over-the-counter and prescription drugs. I think we have to think in much broader terms. We are an addictive society with a great many addictions that are not recognized.

I believe that anything that interferes in our relationships and communications with people in our world should be considered addictions.

We already have names for some of these addictions. The workaholic is recognized and even admired. The long work day is accepted as the road to success but they often preclude family intimacy. Unless the recognition that the family requires time and attention, the workplace can become the place to avoid responsibility for spending valuable time building family relationships that will affect members the rest of their lives.

The person who makes money a top priority may be a workaholic or someone who stretches ethics beyond what is honest and fair in order to have the money. The Wall Street brokers and the Savings and Loan officers might be examples.

The person who uses sex as a substitute for a relationship with a person has an addiction. We have reached the place where sex is considered an introductory step when meeting someone new rather than the celebration of a successful relationship. It becomes a conquest and often doesn't develop beyond a very superficial level. We have not learned how to express ourselves in such a way to communicate who we are as persons.

When we go to the medicine or liquor cabinet, our modeling gives the message that something outside ourselves will "fix" whatever ails us, which is reinforced by television. Prescription and over-the-counter drugs are a multi-million dollar business. There is something that is supposed to fix anything that is wrong is the message. Soft drinks and junk foods make us "feel" better. Obesity is a national problem in spite of desperate efforts to keep the youthful figure that is admired.

No wonder our children are angry and striking out at this social system that doesn't value their worth and respect each individual's "personhood".

"An unexamined life is not worth living" is a concept that is a few thousand years old. It still has an important message for us. We need to examine our lifestyles and what might be our addictions. What kind of messages are we giving to our children? What are our priorities?

Without thinking, we give our children messages that discount their personhood. We may be too busy with business, doing housework, fixing the car, getting the lawn mowed, and the hundreds of homely tasks necessary to maintain a household. It is important to convey to our partners and children that our relationship with them is of top priority.

While eating out recently, I noticed a couple waiting for the hostess to seat them. The man was talking on his telephone, continuing his conversation while the hostess took them to their table. I wondered what his companion was feeling. Don't you suppose that he might have an addiction?

After a talk I gave to new parents on what our wee ones are learning, a middle-aged man came up afterward to share that his older children were grown but he was expecting a new baby soon. He indicated that he was impressed with all that children were learning during their early years and expressed regret that his reactions with his older children had been quite different. He held out his hand and said, "Look at the size of that hand! I like to work on cars, but if one of my children interfered I just whammed them with that. I did not know what I was doing." He was earnest in his wish to be a different father this time around.

It may be as simple as responding differently in each situation than is our habit. Instead of "I'm busy now," we might invite them to join us because we like to have them with us. Instead of "Go clean your room," we might say, "It is such fun to be with you, I'll help you clean your room if you will help me clean mine."

It probably means learning how to have a weekly family conference in order to discuss our feelings regarding what has happened during the week. It is important to talk about the good and the uncomfortable, with particular attention to how we may encourage the good feelings and resolve the distressful. It means suspending judgement and allow each to vent whatever they are feeling with complete confidence that solutions will be discussed and followed through with an evaluation of success the following week. We can list the tasks of the family and each choose ones for which we will be responsible. It means we can share budget priorities after essential expenses are met. Children will grow up understanding more about the monetary cost of being a family, as well as how to communicate more effectively as a family.

"You know, mother, you choose all the neat things to do around the house and make us do the boring things." Our middle daughter said to me one day.

Surprised, I asked what she meant.

"Oh, you get the meals and make us do the dishes." Well, that was certainly true. I asked if she would like to get the meal and she said she would love to. I agreed to trade responsibilities. Soon, Kathy was planning and fixing elaborate meals. I sometimes viewed the kitchen afterward with dismay. Now she is a gourmet cook, using cooking as her means of relaxation. She also cleans up as she cooks!

A young family I had contact with during my years as a parent educator, invited me to dinner. The mother explained that it was the second grader's turn to cook and he certainly prepared a tasty meal. The mother pointed out that if I had come on the night when it was the kindergartner's turn, I probably would have had hot dogs.

Family conferences can provide the respect each person needs to achieve a sense of belonging and sharing.

One of the examples given in Life In The Classroom by Philip Jackson points out the different message a teacher gives between expecting the textbook answer and an interest in that particular student's answer. There is a profound difference between the message "I am only interested in the 'right' answer" and the message given when the teacher is truly interested in knowing what each student is thinking about the question and genuinely wanting to know why he is thinking that way. The students recognize the difference. Jackson indicates a probable thousand interchanges a day between teacher and students that either reinforce self-esteem or diminish it.

Let us recognize that we are the models, we are giving messages all the time and we must examine what kind of messages we are giving our partners and our children. We must examine our addictions, explore why we are addicted, and overcome our addictions so that we can build responsible, fun, and satisfying relationships with our families, friends and work associates. We must quit driving our children crazy with our addictions!

We Drive Our Kids Crazy When We Sexually Molest Them

"Men have strong sexual drives and a good wife should learn to respond to that need," was the advice I received at the time of my marriage. It was during World War II and I was in love and totally committed to being the best wife ever. I understood that I also needed to put my husband first if I were to be a good mother which was a part of my "career" choice. The best wife and mother was a common goal for women of that time.

When my husband left for overseas, his father, in the only intimate conversation we ever had, "hoped I would meet his son's sexual needs and not deprive him as his wife had." Horrified, that he would even think I would deprive my husband of anything, I again committed myself to the "best wife" concept.

When the war was over and the inevitable separations had ceased, we settled down to a life together. After several years of togetherness and two children, I explained to my husband that I thought I could be responsive and enjoy our intimate relationship a few times a week, but I was feeling used when it was occurring several times a night. I needed him to choose which he preferred. His only response was to continue the established pattern. I thought, as a good wife, that I had no choice. It took me many years to understand how devastating and destructive that was to our relationship as well as our family's.

Fifty years later, understanding of positive sexual relationships is still not understood and probably contributes to the sexual abuse so prevalent in our society today.

One can hardly read the daily paper without reading about some abuse that has taken place. There is speculation whether it is a newly developing phenomena or a recently revealed one.

The statistics regarding child sexual abuse are unbelievable: 1 in 3-4 girls; 1 in 7-10 boys; approximately 80-90% of the offenders are known to the abused children and 1/2 of them are fathers or stepfathers. A high percentage of prostitutes are the victims of incest.

It is not something we can say won't happen to us. The statistics belie that. I believe it is a cultural disease.

If that many children had any other disease, we would be frantically looking for some way to prevent it. We are just beginning to expose the extent of the problem and the facts are shocking!

The perspective from history may lead to some explanation though certainly no excuse. For thousands of years in our western culture women and children were considered property to be used as males wanted.

Many of these attitudes (male, of course) are interpretations of the Bible.

Woman was made from man. Women were created for men. (1 Cor. 11:7) "Wives be subject to your husbands." (Ephesians 6:22) In the year 584 AD. a discussion was held on the question "Are women human?" When the issue was voted on, it won by one vote!

When you think it was just in this century that women in our United States of America have had the right to vote, it is easy to understand how recently women were considered property to be treated as the male "owner" wished.

Not all cultures have a problem with sexual abuse. In cross-cultural studies, it was found that in 47% of countries studied, rape was absent or rare. Why is this so? It was concluded that rape is not a biological drive but a learned response which comes from the way society is organized.

The societies that encourage men and boys to be tough, aggressive, competitive, and that tolerate violence are usually societies that trace their beginnings to male supremacy. In rape-free societies women are respected as influential members of society.

"Boys will be boys" has been a powerful excuse for generations.

Our historical heritage is that women are to be used and in spite of the movement toward equality, we are a long way from overcoming that attitude.

As our awareness of sexual molestation is becoming more widespread, we are learning more about the offenders.

The current stereotype of the rapist is the dirty, sleazy, sex-starved man. A quote from <u>Misunderstandings About Sex Criminals</u>: "The sexual offender may be:

• Passive and inhibited

• Active and assertive

• Gentle or violent,

• Religious or irreligious,

• Masculine or effeminate.

• He may hate his mother, love his mother, or be ambivalent about her.

• He may have had a repressive sexual development or he may have been overstimulated.

We could continue with these kinds of comparisons, however, what there is in common, is a serious defect in the interpersonal relationships, an absence of mature, selfless concern for the victim of his obsession, an inability to love in a desexualized manner, a terrible sadness and sense of loneliness, and a totally self-centered orientation."

When so many children are molested, we need to understand that such violence *is* a cultural disease of epidemic proportions.

A majority of sex offenders experienced abuse in their own development. They may be acting out sexual offenses experienced as children. They have learned early to bury deep within because they thought there was no one to tell or were strictly warned not to tell. They often learned to hide *all* their feelings. As a result, when they grow up, they are very adept at hiding and avoiding thinking about what happened to them and what they are doing to their children. "The sins of our fathers..."

An offender often espouses a strict moral code and is usually critical of others but is often limited in his ability to exhibit TRUST and EMPATHY. His relationships lack intimacy, emotion, and openness. Offenders seldom tell the truth about their behavior. They will minimize, deny, and lie about what happened. This is especially true for child molesters:

- "Oh, nothing really happened...
- I was just giving him a bath...
- Don't believe the kid...
- She doesn't know what she is talking about...
- I was drunk, I don't remember a thing."

They seldom express remorse or any sense that what they did was wrong. They will be most concerned with the consequences facing them once they are caught. In this regard, they can be very manipulative of those around them. They are usually repeat offenders and will continue to abuse until they are stopped. Offenders are often passing on their own exploitation because they haven't dealt with the anger that is buried deep within.

One of the most tragic aspects of sexual abuse, is society tends to blame the victim, although we deny this. (A recent local case where the father, a high level state employee, was acquitted of sexually molesting his daughter. His sixteen year old daughter was an alcoholic and was promiscuous so, it was argued, she couldn't be believed. The reporters didn't report a possible connection between her problems and the abuse).

The father, teacher, doctor, or priest is "too nice to do that. Why he is a pillar of the church. He is respected in the community. I can't believe he would do such a thing. She can't be telling the truth.

- She must have asked for it...
- She shouldn't have been in that neighborhood...
- It's the clothes she wears." (Misunderstandings About Sex Criminals)

Why do we blame the victim? I believe our whole society makes the innocent, victims! We start with infants. We tell them once or twice and then expect them to have learned.

"Don't touch! You are old enough to know better." Then we slap their hands and scold. I just heard yesterday about a woman who punished her thirteen month old with "time out". We begin to make them victims.

During the second year, children are developing autonomy. They are exploring their sense of self, their independence with frequently expressed

NO. Often our reaction is, "Don't say no to me." We tell them in one way or another that saying no is not allowed. Often we learn that lesson well. Too many of us grow up unable to say no when it may be important; in the back seat of a car, to a drug offer, to an invitation to the tenth committee that takes us away from our families. Learning it is alright to "just say no" is more complex than we have thought.

Another way we teach small children to be victims seems innocuous and little girls are particularly vulnerable. "Let's look pretty for daddy, let's clean up the house for daddy," "let's wait on daddy."

As I mentioned before, our oldest daughter had been chosen as her school's second exchange student to Japan. When her younger sister and I drove her to San Francisco where she was to board ship, Nancy was looking more and more serious. Kathy, seeking to cheer her up, said "Just think, Nancy, you won't have to get Daddy a cup of coffee for a whole year!" Shocked and surprised, I had to rethink the value of having our children at their Dad's beck and call.

Children first encounter violence in their homes with the people who love them. While they are learning to live in their world, we blame them if they don't measure up to our expectations, which are often unrealistic, because we haven't learned how children grow and develop. We should rather examine *how* we tell them and *why* they don't want to cooperate. Children want to please and feel a real need to please the people on whom they are totally dependent. Most of us wouldn't want to cooperate if we were treated as we often treat children.

Children begin to develop a sense of self and that they are separate from their mothers during the early years of life. They are developing independence and the desire to do for themselves. If parents don't recognize the importance of that development and limit and punish, children become angry and frustrated which is released in temper tantrums. Often biting is about the only weapon they have where they can defend themselves and, of course, they are punished when they do that.

We need to examine why they are angry and eliminate the causes. Children do so want to please. If they are angry, it is important to examine ourselves and what we are doing to cause the anger.

It is imperative that we examine our parenting and teaching methods, as well as our society and search for the reason there is so much anger that leads to so many abuses. Much of it is beginning in those early infant toddler years as adults ignore how children are feeling and expect behavior children are incapable of achieving.

We blame the children rather than assume the responsibility to examine the environment. We blame the children rather than the system when they don't succeed in school. The youngster in the slow reading group is a victim. It is the child's fault that he (usually a little boy) is not reading at grade level. Our school system is programming six year old victims. The primary teacher's self-esteem depends on success at teaching reading. It is easier to blame the children, (it *must* be their fault) since the children in the top group are reading. One-hundred and eighty days in the slow reading group undermines self-esteem and they begin to see themselves as failures.

When children are five, six, and seven there can be close to a year's difference in chronological age. Maturation levels can be very different. Each child may have different strengths, but not necessarily ones that the schools reinforce. The reading groups were developed to recognize those differences, but the goals remained the same. Maturation is more important than I.Q. at those ages. The system turns six year olds into failures and the anger children feel is internalized.

They develop an anger and bitterness toward the unfairness with no way to express it. It builds on the anger that is already there. They are developing a lack of trust and empathy, as well as a lack of conscience, the very same lacks found in sexual offenders and others who are striking out at the unfairness. These children are growing up to be teachers, religious leaders, athletes, and fathers but they are picking up very destructive feelings that are never dealt with. We *are* driving our children crazy. They grow up to be "crazy" adults under a pose of respectability.

Violence is tolerated, even sought out and enjoyed on the ever-present television and movie screens. The United States is one of the world leaders in the amount of violence depicted on screens. Sexually explicit films are checked out for viewing on VCR's with children in attendance.

Even if you don't show them in your home you can not be sure your children are not seeing them.

One of my friends with small children discovered such an incident when her five year old asked questions regarding a sexually explicit act. She brought it up a number of times the following week, puzzling her parents. Later, the mother learned that a neighboring family had been viewing such a film in the middle of the afternoon with their children as well as the neighbor children present.

We need to examine our own need for violent and sexually explicit films. Do they relieve our own anger and bitterness that we have within us? Even if our children are safely in bed, we need to examine our need for such films. The ancient creed, "Know thyself" is indeed relevant. Why do we have such a need to view such films? We are the models for our children. They will become like us!

Destructive family relationships provide negative models and contribute to lack of TRUST and EMPATHY. Compassion and sensitivity are learned by being treated with compassion and sensitivity. With the high rate of divorce indicating deteriorating relationships, it is not easy to model support and understanding, particularly when most of us haven't had support and understanding ourselves.

There are families with his children, her children, and their children trying to live together. Everyone needs positive family relationships but there is little preparation for the social and emotional impacts on marriage and family. When the couples with their own children are not succeeding in families, the blended families have a monumental task to achieve harmony. It is easy to understand how a terrible sadness and sense of loneliness could develop.

If we are going to have any hope of eliminating sexually-related crime, the "R" for Relationships must take precedence over the reading, 'riting, 'rithmetic "R's". I think children will learn those 3 "R's" more successfully, also.

We are going to have to find ways to firmly limit without verbally or physically violating our little ones and undermining their TRUST,

EMPATHY, COMPASSION, AND SENSITIVITY so they can develop intimacy, emotional stability, and an openness in their relationships.

We are going to have to understand and appreciate how much they are learning at very early age and be sure it enhances self-esteem and does not make them victims.

We are going to have to listen to them with understanding hearts. We are going to have to be sensitively aware of what we are teaching them. We are going to have to quit making victims of the innocent.

We are going to have to become comfortable with our own sexuality. That is probably one of the most difficult tasks we have. In many ways we have been taught not to deal with our sexual feelings in respectful and appropriate ways. We start with infants when we play games with them. Where are your toes, fingers, nose, but never the penis or vulva. They begin to learn early that we don't talk about that. Later, when they ask questions they sense our discomfort and don't ask again.

When our oldest son was grown, he told me about how he remembered I had handled his question regarding masturbation. When he mentioned it, I did remember. He remembered that I said, "Don't worry about it, all little boys do it." But he added that he also knew I was uncomfortable about it and didn't bring it up again. I had read the books and knew what I wanted to say but my body language spoke so loudly, that the wrong message was clear to him. "Don't talk about it." The message I had received throughout my growing up years was recycled through in spite of more enlightened information.

We have much to accomplish as adults if we are to give children an appreciation of their own sexuality. We have to be comfortable teaching about "good touch and bad touch" if we are going to help them learn to be discriminating. We have so much to learn ourselves in order to model positive sexuality.

We are going to have to make husband and wife relationships a top priority. When we learn to relate with intimacy and openness, we will exhibit trust, empathy, compassion, and sensitivity. We will have to model these qualities. Our children will be like us.

I just read this morning that William Lederer, a matrimonial authority, says that eighty percent of all marriages in the United States are bad. He states, "electing accuracy over delicacy: Hardly anyone marries when they're in love, just when they're in heat."

We must eliminate the terrible sadness and sense of loneliness that comes when we don't have someone close. When there are so many child-abuse cases, it indicates that many of us have serious defects in our interpersonal relationships. We have to assume the responsibility to change ourselves.

A regional manager of a local company emphasizes that the employees should be sure to have time for their partners and children. He maintains that the staff should be taking their spouses on romantic dates at least once a week. More managers should be that concerned. The future of business and industry depends on the kind of leaders these children will grow up to be, so there is a vested interest.

It takes time and effort to build positive relationships and we must learn how to do it. It doesn't just happen and it will not be easy. It is difficult to continue the "courting" relationship with the pressures of daily living, but unless it is understood as a priority it will never happen. We slide out of romantic courting attitudes as we struggle with learning to be a mother and father. By far the most important thing we can give our children is two parents who love each other and are able to demonstrate it. Unless we are able to build positive relationships with our partners, we will not be adequate models for our children. They will be like us.

A perceptive fifth grader was quoted in <u>About Ourselves</u> by Overstreet.

> With half a laugh of hearty zest,
> I strip me off my coat and vest-
> Then heeding not the frigid air.
> I fling away my underwear.
> So having nothing else to doff,
> I rip my epidermis off-.

More secrets to acquaint you with.

I pare my bones to strips of pith-

And when the expose' is done-

I hang, a cobweb skeleton.

While there you sit aloof remote-

And will not shed your overcoat.

Could there be a more delightful way to invite one to come across, to share one's feelings, to communicate?

In addition to being "good" models, we must give children the information they need regarding good touch and bad touch. When our children were small, I tried hard to understand the balance between warning about strangers without developing unreasonable fears. When one daughter was in the third grade, a sheriff visited all the classrooms at school, handing out flyers warning of strangers, because someone had picked up a child going home from school. Our older daughter had been offered a ride but turned him down. She was asked to describe the person. During all the excitement, her younger sister exclaimed, "I'm glad this happened!" Shocked, I asked why. "Because now I know you weren't just kidding."

We have to examine the messages we give small children because unless they experience TRUST, EMPATHY, COMPASSION, AND SENSITIVITY, they will not develop those qualities. If they are building anger toward that adult world "up there", they will take vengeful action toward others or seek to try to destroy themselves. Suicide is the second cause of death (after auto accidents) in young people and we don't know how many try and don't succeed.

Unless we are able to examine our past and consciously retrieve those old "tapes" in our subconscious, recognize the need for changing our attitudes, and model positive relationships, developing TRUST, EMPATHY, INTIMACY, and OPENNESS in our relationships we will not eliminate this cultural disease of sexual, verbal, and physical abuse that is so destructive of children and ourselves. It is imperative that we assume responsibility to stop this tragic pattern, or we will continue to drive our children crazy.

We Drive Our Kids Crazy Unless We Are Playful

When our oldest daughter was twelve, she was lost overnight on a rock-hunting trip in the mountains. I won't ever forget the agony of those long hours. Without consciously realizing it at the time, it was that night that I decided I had to be a more "careful" mother and lost my playfulness. For a long time I wasn't aware that it was gone and now find it difficult to regain. I do firmly believe that playfulness and a light touch is a vital ingredient in families.

Years after that traumatic night, a Transactional Analysis professor helped me to understand the subconscious decision I had made. It was result of a message that had been a part of my childhood life decisions. What we learn in the cradle, goes with us to the grave. My mother had often shared the following quote, "Be good, sweet maid, and let who will be clever. Do noble things, don't dream them all day long. And thus make life, death, and that vast forever, one grand sweet song." I had subconsciously decided that when Nancy was lost I had not been "good enough" or life would be a song. So, in order to make life a grand sweet song, I would have to be a "gooder" mother.

As we earnestly try to fulfill our roles as parents, we often become absorbed in doing a "good" job and forget the value of playfulness. The importance of the "light touch," maintaining or developing a sense of humor in our interactions with our children, is an essential ingredient of parenthood. Since parenting is an art rather than a science, and *no* one has been able to develop "right" ways to parent, I think that we can view each situation with a sense of humor and realize that it is the total climate of respect for the personhood of children that is important.

I feel the need to distinguish between teasing that can be destructive and playfulness which is appreciated. Teasing is often considered playfulness, but I don't believe it is the same. Each can be measured by the way one feels during the encounter. Playfulness will lead to a more loving warm regard while teasing often is damaging. The teaser will often couch a criticism in teasing terms. The person who is teased (teasee?) will sense the "put down" intended and may react to it. The teaser will then blame them for poor sportsmanship. "Can't you take a joke?" or "I am only teasing," which they think negates their responsibility for the destructiveness of the interaction. It doesn't resolve the problem that the criticism implied.

We need to watch for the "stars in their eyes". If the "stars" are there, it is playfulness. This is true of our partners, as well as our children. If hurt replaces the "stars" it is destructive. If someone teases others in negative ways, it often means they don't feel very good about themselves and feel a need to destroy good feelings in others.

Most parents are concerned about the teasing that goes on in their family because they sense its danger. I know, as a young parent, I interrupted my older three children whenever there was teasing. *We were not going to have teasing in our family!* It seemed to get more intense as the children grew older and I was always in there as referee.

By the time the younger two came along, I knew what I had been doing didn't work so I tried to stay out of their interactions with each other. I made a special effort to avoid involvement in the teasing episodes. It was one of the most difficult changes in me that I have had to make. I had to bite my tongue or leave the room. "He's going to make her cry—he's going too far—now she's crying." is a sample of the internal dialogues I held with myself. But I avoided interfering. Then Chip would say, "Aw, Stacy, if you can't tease your sister who can you tease?" and Stacy would be right back for more. It was most amazing! As a result, there was an elimination of destructive teasing between the two. I was impressed with the discovery that our children can handle their relationships just fine, if we free them to do so.

The single example that impressed me the most was the time Chip, then a senior in high school, had planned a rock-climbing expedition with his friends, all boys. Stacy, who is four years younger than her brother, asked if she could go along.

"Sure," said Chip and she went. Needless to say, I was impressed and thrilled and *at that moment* I felt like I was a successful parent. It was worth all the times I had to work so hard at avoiding interference.

Parents sometimes tease their children and each other in destructive ways.

"I'm going to trade you in on a new model!" jokingly said by my husband at moments he felt I had failed him in some way was terribly hurtful. I tried to laugh it off because he was just "teasing" but the hurt is still there. I needed reassuring playfulness at those times.

Teasing is not playfulness.

We are learning so much without our conscious knowledge and it affects us all our lives. Since many young parents have not had much experience with new babies, a playful outlook may not be automatic. Those new babies look so fragile. Developing a more relaxed attitude that encourages laughter and playfulness should be a priority. Understanding the concept of discipline that reinforces self-esteem can free the playfulness within us. Limits can be enforced with a sense of empathetic humor, which will help gain cooperation.

When we realize misbehavior is an experiment with learning, and each of us have a lifetime for growth, we can allow playfulness to become that vital ingredient in parenthood.

One of the parents in the Parent Cooperative Program at the community college came to me for help with a seminar on playfulness. She shared this story.

During the Christmas holidays, her husband had suggested taking the children to slide in the park.

"Oh, you go, dear, I'm busy." was her automatic reply. He accused her of not appreciating the "co-op" philosophy. Since she was very active in the program, she bristled and asked him what he meant. He replied that the co-op advocated taking time with your children.

"Oh, alright, I'll go." was her impatient reply.

They went to the park and she stood shivering while the father and two children went sliding down the hill. After the first slide, they came excitedly running to her urging her to come with them because it was so much fun. Reluctantly, with a sense of duty, she agreed and joined them.

It was fun! She said the rest of the afternoon she played as eagerly as the children did. She gained an important understanding. How differently both she and the children felt when she joined *their* play and truly shared the enjoyment *with* them. What a different message from standing aside, shivering while supervising them. She wanted to develop their next parent meeting to share her insights.

We need to look for all the opportunities to share the fun rather than to just supervise their play (and work).

Another form of teasing that can be harmful, is tickling and wrestling. Gentle tickling and wrestling is wonderful fun. It is imperative to keep it fun for the children. When the laughter becomes hysterical or anger develops in the wrestling, we have not been gentle enough. It is not something that children should learn to be good sports about. It is especially important that parents don't overdo this kind of teasing with their children.

A good measure of successful playfulness will be that feelings between you will be warm and appreciative. Teasing will foster animosity, often taking it out on others later. It drives our kids crazy. An attitude of playfulness and taking time to share their play will keep the "stars" in their eyes.

We Drive Our Kids Crazy With Christmas

A Dennis the Menace cartoon showed Dennis viewing all the presents under the tree on Christmas morning and saying, "All of this!" After all the gifts were opened, he is shown asking, "Is this all?"

How many times in one form or another do we ask, "Is this all?" Often our actual experiences don't live up to our expectations.

Our talk AND planning AND activity involved in Christmas preparations are overwhelming to children. It takes a lot of time, energy, and effort to prepare for the holidays, often at the expense of children's REAL needs. The streets, stores, TV, radio, churches, and schools all indicate something special is going to happen. It all focuses on the gifts of Christmas.

The gifts are the material representation of the meaning of Christmas just as the Wise Men brought their gifts of gold, frankincense, and myrrh. The Wise Men's gifts were the material symbols recognizing the birth of a King. A King who brought a message of LOVE. We mustn't allow that message to be diminished into "things".

During the courtship a man and woman exchange rings as symbols representing their love and promise. The ring would be meaningless without the love it represents. Marriage is the result of that love. The divorce rate represents the number of people who later asked, "Is this all?" When the occasions of anger, sarcasm, and boredom outweigh the "gifts" of love, thoughtfulness, and concern, a meaningless marriage or divorce results. Is this all? Each of us need more than this, but we haven't learned how to love.

I think Dennis recognized there is more to Christmas than the material gifts lying under the tree and was honest about it. Is this all?

All that fuss for *this*!

We parents want to give our children all we can and realize that the important gifts cannot be wrapped in tinsel and fancy paper to be torn off in haste. We love our children but find it difficult to send "love" messages when children are not behaving in socially acceptable ways, often as a result of the pressures on the family as they get ready for holidays.

The opportunity to understand that either verbal or physical violence violates the message of love hasn't been internalized. Children are sensitive and need messages of loving support while they learn society's rules, limits, and disciplines. The recognition that children can learn the necessary limits without violating them as people (such as using punishment) has been long in developing.

Overcoming old attitudes and learning loving ways of relating to children takes self-discipline. I am responsible for me and if the relationship with my child is not a positive one, I need to examine me and my ways of reacting rather than blame the child and his behavior. I am the adult who is to provide the positive learning environment so children will want to cooperate.

Christmas is a special time of the year for many people! To many it represents the season of giving—or getting?

It is so much fun to watch the children open their gifts—giving or getting?

It is a joy to have the family together—giving or getting?

And yet Christmas is for many, many people a time of depression. Isn't it a shame to mention *that* regarding this joyous season? Is there any connection between the hectic pace to get ready for Christmas and that depression? Do you suppose that when children are tired, hurt, or angry, that we too busy to be gentle, loving, and understanding?

When I am in department stores, I sense the tension and importance of the visit with Santa. Whose need is being met? Are we giving—or getting?

Are *we* so anxious for pictures with Santa that we don't listen to our children express their anxiety and fears of sitting on this funny-looking stranger's lap? Do we rush around shopping, dragging tired children or leave them with strangers in nurseries?

What is the true meaning of Christmas? We certainly don't want our children to grow up to be "depressed" statistics at Christmas time.

As parents of young children, let's give our children during the days before Christmas a most important gift—the gift of some relaxed time each day with them. We will be giving—*and* getting!

Can we check out our "giving" time each night before we go to sleep? How much special time did we give each member of the family this day? Do we go to sleep with positive feelings toward our families or are we too tired, too busy, too harried?

Christmas is love. It can be a beautiful time to renew family relationships. Our Christmas traditions need to generate love. I believe it is important to understand me and respect my needs if I am to be able to "love my neighbor (my child) as myself." I think our Christmas traditions need to do that if we are to eliminate future depression at Christmas time. (There is some indication that all the sweets and treats affect our systems to cause some of the depression. Should that be a warning in evaluating our new traditions)?

Let us not blindly follow tradition but develop new traditions that make Christmas a joyous season with positive ways of spending family time that will last all year.

Each of our holiday celebrations can be examined and discussed as a family. What is the meaning for this holiday? How can we best celebrate that meaning so it becomes meaning-full in a personal way. Traditions are an important part of building "family". Exploring what traditions have meant and choosing worthwhile "old" ones but establishing exciting new ones can be a positive way of building "family". When the holiday is over, we hope it will be one of the warm memories that will be shared throughout the years and passed down to our children's children, because they meant so much.

On Christmas night we do *not* want to feel, "Is this all?"

It would be great to feel: "This has been the most wonderful Christmas ever!!!"

We Drive Our Kids Crazy Unless We Model Healthy Living

"Mommy, I don't want to eat this icky stuff!"

What do we do? When I was growing up, our generation was often told to think of the starving children in India and clean up our plates.

"Clean up your plate and you can have your dessert," is another old-fashioned reply. At least, I hope we have out-grown it. I am sure it has contributed to our national obesity problem. Many of us feel we deserve our dessert if we ate our meal, no matter how satiated we are.

Adults usually prepare foods they prefer but expect children to eat what has been prepared.

"See, daddy cleans his plate." How often is food served that daddy doesn't like?"

Children seem to have been born with an understanding of what their bodies need. Too often, we interfere and damage their sensitivity to what their bodies are telling them.

Remember, what I said about spoiling babies? We can't do it. I want to remind you about the story of our fourth child from a nutrition standpoint. When he was a brand new infant (about ten days old), the doctor suggested I start feeding cereal. (He is 32 years old now, so it has been awhile). As it seemed to upset Chip, the doctor suggested I start trying different kinds of cereal. In retrospect, I wish I had just quit all cereal for a period. (I was still doing what the doctor told me to do at that time, instead of evaluating his suggestions and exploring answers for myself.) Instead, we began to try each kind of baby cereal available to find something that wouldn't cause tummyaches. When I quit nursing our baby, with the doctor's encouragement since he thought it could be my milk, the problem seemed to worsen. I spent a great amount of time rocking and comforting this wee one, with the constant accusation that I was spoiling him.

When Chip was eighteen months old, a dietician friend read in her professional journal that there was a high amount of linoleic acid in breast milk which was not in other foods that babies ate. My doctor said a spoonful of corn or soy bean oil was just a food and wouldn't hurt him. It would certainly be better than the prescribed medicine he was getting.

Overnight, there was decided improvement and Chip was delighted to be free to play. He was no longer a fussy, hurting baby and I felt no need to hold him. He was happy to play when he didn't have the tummyaches. If I would forget to give him the spoonful of oil, he would come and ask for it. I decided that if, in addition, I alternated his foods so that he only received the same food every fourth day, it might help to avoid the tummyaches. I was amazed to see the differences a spoonful of corn oil could make.

I learned several very important lessons. You don't spoil babies when you hold them when they hurt and there is much we don't understand regarding the chemistry of our bodies. Do remember this story when you are comforting a hurting child.

Many (at least 25) years later, I was speaking at a University to a parent group. One mother came up to apologize for bringing her baby, but he was so fussy and uncomfortable that she didn't like leaving him with a sitter. I empathized with her, remembering Chip's situation. When she described her baby's symptoms, I told her about Chip and the corn oil. I told her that I had a copy of the the article and if she or her doctor wanted to see it, I would send her a copy. A week later, I received a relieved, grateful letter. The baby was very much improved and her doctor wanted to see the article.

When our next baby was tiny, I offered only breast milk with no supplemental foods until she was nearly five months old. She was the happiest, most contented baby we had.` No colic, no need for constant comfort, and so very healthy. `She was four years old before she had her first cold.

These experiences have been responsible for my fervent belief that we must listen very carefully to what our babies tell us. I think it might be wise to offer breast milk (it really is the healthiest, as well as, the easiest way to feed a baby) to new babies waiting for some indication on the infant's part as to when he will be ready for something more. Pay close attention to what they tell us. It might, also, be wise to alternate the foods when we do begin additional foods. We may be building allergies by offering the same food daily. It probably would be best for all of us to avoid eating many of the same foods more frequently than every four days. Certainly, allergies are a serious problem for many adults.

My experiences with our five children have helped me to understand the importance of paying close attention to them. Of course, it has taken five children plus an additional 20 years of working with parents to learn this. I am hoping to share with you and possibly prevent the anxiety and anguish that I suffered through the years.

Parents spend so much time preparing and feeding babies during the first year that they are not prepared for how much food toddlers can stow away very quickly, when they are able to feed themselves. For example, compare the time it takes to give an infant a bottle and how quickly milk can disappear when the child can drink it "all by myself" (Of course, sometimes it gets spilled.) It is such a sudden change from the time it has taken to feed an infant, that often parents don't believe they are getting enough to eat and try to push more food.

Babies usually triple their birth weight during the first year. They only gain a couple of pounds the second year. A relaxed attitude with trust that the child will eat what is needed will make these toddler years more pleasant and avoid pitting the child against the parent and the parent against the child, which so often happens.

We can seat children in high chairs, but we are unable to make them eat, unless we force feed, which they can promptly throw up. We can put children to bed, but we cannot make them go to sleep. We can seat children on toilets, but we cannot make them "go". It is an excellent parenting policy to avoid conflicts over those issues, because the parents will lose.

Learn to trust that children will know what should be eaten, (it has been shown that the child may be allergic to the food refused).

Arrange a time for bed, but give children the freedom to decide when to go to sleep. A light close to the bed and interesting quiet activities can keep a child happy until they choose to turn off the light and go to sleep.

Observing children carefully, we will discover clues that will guide us in responding to their toileting needs. `My children showed me that it took them less than a week, when they were in charge.

Many conflicts can be avoided, if we are sensitive to our children and are relaxed and trusting.

Every child recognizes the "Golden Arches". At the end of the day, if both parents are working outside the home, it is a welcome sign for parents, too. Responding to public pressure, McDonald's has offered salads and low fat shakes. (I am not sure about the effect of artificial sugars on small bodies.) The popularity of hamburgers, french fries, milk shakes, and soft drinks has not diminished. We attended a movie recently and a youngster who couldn't have been more than eight years old was buying a quart size Pepsi. I wonder what that much sugar and caffeine was doing to his system.

Many doctors and nutritionists believe the rapidly increasing number of "hyperactive" children is directly related to the fats, sugars, salt, and caffeine intake of children. (TV is also considered a culprit). There has been documentation of the connection between caffeine, anxiety, and depression. When children drink soft drinks they are taking in much more caffeine, sugar, as well as artificial sugars, per pound of body weight than adults. The organs of their bodies are exposed to much greater concentrations of these substances. Certainly, it will affect a thirty pound body much more seriously than a hundred and thirty pound body.

When adults are constantly warned about the effects of these foods on their health and weight, it does seem we should be more concerned about what our children are eating and model for them (and ourselves) more responsible eating habits.

Obesity has become a national menace and children are particularly vulnerable. A Michigan State University study indicated that heredity is responsible for about 12% of the children who are overweight. They need special help to overcome their obesity but all children need their "significant adults" to model healthy eating.

Our adult concern with weight and health problems, indicates the difficulty people of this nation have with changing food habits. We are not as active as we once were, but are still eating the same way. Let's get off our kid's backs and model responsible patterns, making dinner time relaxed and fun.

Our kids will become like us.

We have not been paying much attention to cholesterol in children, because we don't expect children to have heart attacks. There is a beginning recognition that checking children's cholesterol makes sense in order to have a base line for future reference. It has been found in recent research that more than two hours of television viewing is closely tied to high cholesterol in children. We should become aware of our own cholesterol, too.

I was talking about nutrition to a parent group, predicting the increase in heart attacks at younger ages.

"Tell me about it! I am only 28 years old and I have just been told by my doctor that unless I change the way I eat, I am a prime candidate for a heart attack soon!" a discouraged young father lamented.

There is some indication that the increased depression at Christmas time comes as a result of the consumption of richer foods that are so prevalent at Halloween, Thanksgiving, Christmas, and New Years. We probably eat more rich foods during those two months than we eat during the rest of the year.

Years ago, Watson reported in <u>Nutrition And The Mind</u> that he was able to help his patients avoid depression during the holiday period by having them maintain their pre-holiday diet, avoiding the rich cuisine.

Seriously, we need to evaluate our holiday celebrations. Too often, serving special food is a major part of any get-together. Time spent with children doing fun activities the whole family can enjoy, might provide happier memories of the holidays than is currently the case.

I think all of us might profit from a less frantic rushing around. If the "tapes in our head" didn't tell us to prepare all that extra food, we would have more time with children. Let the whole family evaluate holiday festivities and everyone have a say in choosing fun responsible ways to celebrate.

The food we eat is a small part of healthy eating. It is important to appreciate the importance of a relaxed, happy time around the table. We think we can hide the unhappy undercurrents between us, as parents, but they speak so loudly that children cannot eat, and, if they do, the food upsets them.

Food eaten when one is upset doesn't do a body much good anyway. An argument between mom and dad can be scary. It may affect the way the child feels about the kind of food that was on the table, the day the argument occurred. He may never be able to eat it again without feeling nauseated, but never understand why that food makes him sick. The family will probably blame it on allergies, and, in a very real way, it is.

Nowadays, when families are spending so little time together, the importance of making the time at the table a happy, relaxed, sharing time cannot be overemphasized. It will mean that mom and dad have to set the pace. *Laughter is the absolutely best ingredient for a happy meal.*

It is important to trust children to eat what they need and when they need it. They are very aware and sensitive to their bodies. It reinforces their self-esteem and allows them to maintain responsibility for themselves.

Children will eat what is needed without direction on our part, if a healthy variety of food is prepared and children are allowed the freedom to choose what to eat from the food prepared. Too often, we fill their plates and tell them to clean them up. Giving very tiny helpings and letting children choose their seconds, if *they* want them, can be much more effective.

"Is this all I get," is a more successful strategy, than "Do I have to eat all of this?" (And we won't have to worry about the wasted food and those starving children in India.)

It takes great responsibility on the parent's part, to maintain a relaxed attitude without pressure, because the powerful messages our parents gave us are so near to the surface. It is always easier to *react* from those "old tapes in our heads" than to *act* with thoughtful consideration responding to the needs of our children.

Our adult requirements (such as enough sleep and time alone together,) will be more easily met, if we can appreciate and respond to our babies appropriately. New babies are demanding! Providing for their physical and emotional needs is exhausting! You wonder if you will *ever* have time for yourself again.

It is reassuring to learn that if those early needs are met during those incredibly important first few months, the child will develop trust that this world is good, that he is important, and will be willing, within a short few months, to begin to learn that others have needs, too. If those needs are not met, babies become more and more demanding, lacking trust in the people around them. When trust does not develop early, it takes much longer to develop later on. An anger and bitterness begins to develop, which leads to the lack of concern for others and precludes conscience development.

It takes great discipline and maturity for young parents to cheerfully meet the demands of wee ones. It is too easy to believe that the " *kids* are driving *us* crazy."

Relaxing and catching up on sleep when that wee one sleeps, is most important. Too often, new parents feel they must catch up on their work during that time. *DON'T!* It will keep, or get someone to help with the work, if you can. You spend your time with your infant. That bonding is vitally important to the family. It is essential to bond with dad, too. The baby *needs* to be held by both mom and dad. Each holds them differently and that is important to their understanding of masculine and feminine and is a major part of bonding.

As we learn to listen actively and sensitively to our babies, we will learn that they have such a beautiful balance in their lives. Small children usually are fairly active if they have the freedom to move. When our oldest was tiny, my ten year old cousin thought our baby didn't get much exercise. I suggested that she lie down on her back and kick and wave and wiggle whenever he did. She was exhausted quickly and decided that Randy was a very active baby.

It is tempting to confine children in playpens to make it easier for us. Freedom to explore their environment is the way they learn about their world and allows the movement necessary to exercise their rapidly developing bodies. Providing exciting new things to explore at floor level can add to the challenge of movement.

It seems to be very difficult for adults to trust that children are learning as much as they do. It is very tempting to *push* rather than *respond*. We start at infancy and it continues through their childhood and adolescence.

So much pressure has been put on children at Little League age, that many kids are burned out by the time they would be ready for high school athletic activities, when they might, more appropriately, be involved in competitive sports.

There are numerous ways to give children ample opportunity to develop skills and get essential exercise without the pressure of competition. It is not the children, who are trying hard to meet their parent's expectations, but their parents and coaches that are the screaming pressures.

When our first son was involved in Little League, he started swearing which was very upsetting to me. When I called him on it, he said the coaches at Little League swore and they went to church so he thought it was alright.

Recently, there have been two newspaper articles that are very disturbing, but they reflect societies' attitudes toward our young ones.

A seventeen year old boy who was a star football player in high school, had a life-threatening health condition that was going to keep him from playing football in college. No doctor would sign the necessary permit. His parents were unhappy with the Athletic Commission's decision, saying their youngster should have the right to make his choice.

If he were allowed to play and something happened to their son, I wonder if they would sue?

The other article featured a star soccer player on a girl's team. Several fathers were so sure that a *girl* could not possibly be so talented; they wanted a "panty check"!

Once children assembled at the neighborhood vacant lot with a ball and bat. They chose up sides and played ball. Often there would be an argument that would lead to disagreement. They would argue and shout and all get mad and go home. Next time, rules would be made that would resolve that issue if it occurred again.

They soon learned that there would be no game if they were angry, breaking up the game, so they gradually developed guidelines that would keep them playing. In addition to developing the physical skills, and getting the exercise they needed, they were developing extremely valuable negotiating and rule-making skills that would serve them in good stead the rest of their lives.

Now adults organize the Little League games, tell children what to do, when, and how to do it, and yell at them if they don't succeed. They have become puppets for the adults to live out their fantasies through their children.

Learning how to respect our children's personhood depends on understanding, respecting, and developing our own personhood, understanding why *we* need to live through our kids.

Ample opportunities for active participation in all kinds of games and skill-developing is essential. Developing habits of physical activity that will keep one interested in maintaining conditioning for the rest of one's life is a part of the balance needed.

Parents who develop a regular exercise routine can include children in a fun way. Children will internalize the importance of daily exercise while performing with their parents. It is fun to do things with them, if unrealistic demands are not imposed.

It has been found that when adults do assume the responsibility of daily exercise, it takes six months to a year of discipline before it becomes a regular part of their lifestyle. Modeling isn't easy. Let's shape up for our kids! (and us).

Providing a balance of the physical, mental, emotional, and spiritual in our daily living is what we need to achieve and will be the best contribution we can make to our children, as well as, keeping us healthy.

Modeling that balance in our own lives is a demanding challenge. It certainly isn't the easiest thing to do, but may keep the pressure off our kids and keep us from driving our children crazy.

We Drive Our Kids Crazy Unless We Are Financially and Politically Responsible

"Daddy, I need a nickel." I asked my father.

"I don't have a nickel," was his casual reply.

"Mommie, I need a nickel," I asked again.

"Honey, I don't have a nickel," was the answer.

"Lucy, I need a nickel," I asked one more time.

"I don't have a nickel." There was no one else to ask.

"My family doesn't have a nickel!" I reported to my first grade teacher, when she was collecting nickels the next morning. That story made it around school quickly because my father was the Superintendent of Schools.

"I just saved you from a Thanksgiving basket the church is sending to the poor!" a neighbor called to tell me. She explained that someone at church had asked all the children's Sunday School classes if they knew anyone who didn't have any money and wasn't going to have turkey for Thanksgiving. My first grade son had raised his hand. The people in the church had called my neighbor to check it out and she had laughingly squelched the idea.

I was horrified, but as I thought about it, I could understand why he had answered that way. We were remodeling our farmhouse, and, after paying our bills and getting food, we would purchase as many building materials as we could afford with what was left. I do know that I wasn't aware enough of the importance of explaining this kind of information to our kids. I just knew we had told our children frequently that we didn't have any money, or that we couldn't afford it.

As for the Thanksgiving turkey, we were going to have duck. Our family was a few states away, I had never prepared duck, a newspaper recipe had sounded good, and it would be plenty for our small family. I promised myself to never talk "poor" again and to be more aware of the money messages we were giving our children.

This same first grader was invited to a birthday party of a friend from school. The child lived across the golf greens in a huge mansion with expansive lawns. Randy had never been in such a fancy house. I worried about how he would feel when he compared this little boy's home with his own. When the chauffeur brought him home, I waited breathlessly for his reaction when I asked him about their house.

"Oh! Mother!" he exclaimed with passion. (Here it comes, I thought.)

"It had Christmas trees all the way around it!"

The first grade teacher asked her students to draw pictures of what their daddy's did for a living. One child had circles drawn all over his page. The teacher asked what his daddy did.

"He makes rounds," the child replied.

Another child had a tree with lots of branches on it.

"What does your daddy do?" asked the teacher.

"He's a branch manager," was the child's answer.

I have told these stories to demonstrate how often we don't look at things from a child's point of view.

I am convinced that ninety per cent of what our children are learning, we would be astounded if we knew that was what we had been teaching, and ninety per cent of what we are deliberately trying to teach, we would be absolutely dumfounded, if we knew what they were really learning. Let us learn to listen to our children.

We are giving messages constantly regarding money.

"What did you spend today? was a part of my father's nightly after dinner ritual. He kept track of everything any of us spent.

When I started school, I received an allowance of a quarter each week. (This was during the depression). One nickel was to go in the bank for college. Another ritual I enjoyed because dad took my hand and we did it together; dad and I would go to my little book bank on mother's bookcase to deposit that nickel. (I was a senior in high school before I learned that everyone did not go to college.)

One nickel went to the Sunday School collection, one nickel was for school supplies, and the remaining dime was mine to spend for anything I wished. I particularly remember delicious cream puffs with powdered sugar on the top that were two for a nickel. Remember, it was during the depression. That is almost unbelievable now, isn't it?

My father paid cash for everything until my mother needed brain surgery. He had a difficult time getting credit because he had no credit rating. He immediately opened several charge accounts, paying promptly on the first of each month. (The store gave a quart of ice cream when bills were paid, which was a special treat for us at that time.)

He saved for our college tuition (which we were required to repay. (He cancelled the $400 I still owed as a part of a wedding gift, when I was married.)

Retirement plans were a very visible and definite part of his savings. He was terribly upset when we went off the gold standard, which he knew would diminish the value of his retirement savings. He believed our country had betrayed us!

The last year he taught school before retirement, teachers were included in the Social Security program. He absolutely hated the idea of accepting it, but he justified it by saying that it was this government's crazy way of making up for the devaluation of the dollar in the years since he had started his retirement program.

As you can recognize, my father was a committed money manager for our family and he has had a measurable impact on me, his oldest daughter.

The *mother* of the man I married paid their bills. You can guess the consequences and understand how I learned much of what is presented in this book.

I think it is necessary to sketch this brief biography of my father because it will give a picture of the attitude of many people before Franklin Roosevelt's social policies were inaugurated, more than fifty years ago.

My father, Charles Randall, arrived at Willamette University with about sixty cents and a motorcycle to attend college. He worked his way through school, often doing dishes for a fraternity. I remember the story of his classmates coming to get him while he was doing dishes because as class president he was to stand in the receiving line of some important activity. They wanted him even if he had to appear in his cords.

As the son of a Methodist minister, he was used to providing for himself or doing without. (Recent research has shown that students who earn their way through college are more successful later on than ones who don't.)

After World War I, he turned down a deserved pension because he believed we are all responsible for keeping our democracy working and the government didn't "owe" us, *we owed* military services *to ourselves* in order to protect *our* country.

He resigned as a Superintendent of Schools with a 25% cut in salary, in order to teach History and Civics. He believed it was important for students to understand the history of our country and how to protect it. He wanted to be a part of that important process and have direct contact with the students.

Franklin Roosevelt's policies during the depression were extremely disturbing to him. I was in high school ('34-'38) and his concerns have made a lasting impression on me.

He was afraid that Social Security would take away a person's incentive to save for a "rainy day". (In spite of the fact that United States citizens have one of the highest standards of living in the world, we now have one of the *lowest* savings rates of any industrialized country.) He believed that by giving money to the government for our retirement (Social Security) we would remove investment money from the private sector. After fifty years, his ideas seem to have been prophetic.

An elderly couple lived in a little house across the street from us. The man was the "handy man" in the neighborhood, doing chores for people who needed help. The neighbors would be sure that he had enough work. When the "New Deal" came along, his wife began complaining that their friends who signed up were getting telephones and she surely would like a telephone. He wasn't going to take "charity" and refused.

She persisted, so with misgivings, he walked the six or eight miles to the center to sign up. Somehow, he felt as if he were being treated as "charity" and walked out in a huff. When his wife continued to nag him, he finally gave up.

During the next few years, he gradually became less and less available for helping the neighbors. He had accepted that the "government owed him a living". My father used that example to emphasize the harm that "welfare" does.

I have included financial and political responsibilities in the same chapter because they are so completely interwoven in the way our attitudes have developed toward money.

I discovered this parody in an old notebook of mine. It is "ages" old. I think it is still very appropriate. I have no information as to the origin or who wrote it. I just know that the notebook contains notes from my very early years.

> "The government is my shepherd
> I need not work.
> It alloweth me to lie down on a good job,
> It leadeth me beside still factories.
> It destroyeth my initiative.
> It leadeth me in the path of a parasite
> For politics' sake.
> Yea, though I walk through the valley of laziness
> And deficit spending,
> I will fear no evil for the government is with me.
> It prepareth an economic Utopia for me,
> By appropriating the earnings of my own grandchildren.
> My inefficiency runneth over.

Surely the government shall care for me
All the days of my life
And I shall dwell in a fool's paradise forever."

I suspect Franklin Roosevelt's policies inspired it.

For fifty years our government has assumed responsibilities that should be ours. I don't think my father's belief system was unusual for people who lived at that time. When government is willing to look after people, it becomes easy to accept it. Three generations have learned to accept it and it has been terribly destructive to their self-esteem. The "in" word today is to "empower" the people, in an effort to overcome the attitude that the government is responsible for us.

My father, reluctantly, justified taking Social Security, even though he had not put money into it, because when our country went off the gold standard, the value of his retirement dollar was reduced. It was so difficult for him to use it, that he would not look at the check when he signed it.

An ancient philosopher predicted that a democracy would last until there were more people getting money from the government than people supporting the government. We might be reaching that place, when we look at the number of entitlement programs. Most of us receive money in some form from the government.

A historian traced the sequence of development of the major civilizations over the centuries. I wish I knew where this came from. I have used it for a number of years and have lost it's source. He indicated people went:

"From bondage to spiritual faith.

From spiritual faith to great courage.

From great courage to liberty.

From liberty to abundance.

From abundance to selfishness.

From selfishness to complacency.

From complacency to apathy.

From apathy to moral decay.

From moral decay to dependency.

From dependency back to bondage."

It is interesting to speculate where we are in that sequence at this time. It is an important reason to learn our history.

Attitudes toward government are developed at home. The adults model responsibility for themselves. The people are the government. We are the country. We allow what is happening. We have to claim the responsibility for ourselves and our government. Whether or not we like what is going on in our government, it is essential to be involved. When such a small percentage of our people vote, it proves that we are not as involved as we should be.

Responsibility for our own economic well-being is an important way to make a difference.

"Pay yourself first!" was the good advice my father gave. He meant it was necessary to put some money aside for savings first, then live on what was left.

"We can't afford it," is the frequent excuse. However, cigarettes, beer, Lotto tickets are some of the items afforded.

Let us model responsible money management for our children (and our country).

Money is a major problem in marriage. "Money is the root of all evil," is an ancient message. Everyone has heard it. It is not money that is the evil, it is our attitude toward money that complicates our lives. Our priorities toward life can be quite different, which means that how we spend money becomes an issue. Each of us wants to spend our money toward our own priorities and conflicts develop when we have differing priorities.

We often go into marriage expecting the lifestyle our parents had achieved after many years of working. Because we were small, it isn't easy to understand or remember the struggles of our parents during their early years of marriage. We want it all at once.

He may want a new car and she may want a new house and neither purchase may be a wise one for them at that time.

Dealing with the differences we bring from each of our families, sharing openly, is one of the beginning ways to build a loving marriage that will have a chance to last. As children arrive, we can develop family councils to share with them the responsibilities of managing a family. When each family finds a means to rely on themselves rather than expect others to assume them, our country will have a chance to get its own house in order.

I was impressed with an outstanding teacher several of my children had in high school. I convinced him we should have an adult class which turned into a great thought-provoking discussion group. The Grand Inquisitor from The <u>Brothers Karamazov</u> was an inspiration to me.

I asked the teacher if he was going to present this chapter to his high school students and if he were, I would surely like to attend. He was and I did.

The Grand Inquisitor was making all the decisions for the people. He said that he had not asked to do it, the people had willingly given the decision making authority to him. They did not want that burden.

The students did understand that then the people began to resent the Grand Inquisitor. The teacher asked the students what would it take to change that. Finally, after much discussion, one student said that you would have to take responsibility for yourself. The teacher popped out of his chair and ran around to pat the student on the back.

"That's right! You have to be responsible, *in the halls, in the senior room, in the back seat of a car!*."

"What was it like today?" the incoming students asked the students who were leaving.

"Oh, it was simply beautiful!" the student beside me exclaimed with a satisfied sigh.

"Boy, have I been working hard, but it sure has been fun!" Kathy, our middle daughter exclaimed, when taking his class. She had just emerged from her room, after spending about three hours alone studying for his class. When teachers challenge, students respond.

Too often, both our homes and schools totally direct the children until they are almost adults and then expect them to take over and *be* responsible without any practice.

The idea that students can decide what to learn, when to learn it, and how to learn it, is absolutely foreign to our thinking.

This has to change, if we are to regain responsibility for ourselves and take it away from the schools and government. We are still caught up in Industrial Revolution thinking, which wanted to train people to get to work at the same time (people had been depending on the sun) and to do what they were told. We have moved into the information age but our school systems have not adapted.

"Will this legislation make people more or less responsible?" should be the main question examined in passing legislation, after including input from the home-crowd.

"Will this decision make students more or less responsible for their own learning?" is the question staff in our schools should be asking, while they involve the students in their decisions.

"Will this direction make our children more or less responsible?" is the question parents can ask, while including their children in the decisions.

Any time we teach something that students can discover for themselves we preclude their understanding.

Self-esteem is tragically undermined each time we take care of someone who can take care of himself, whether children or adults.

Managing money is one of the major ways we can take care of ourselves. If we pay ourselves first, as my father suggested, we can appreciate the value of compound interest. We learned about compound interest in grade school, but to identify personally with it, taking advantage of it, isn't a routine part of either the school's or the home's teaching. We don't relate to it in a way to make it a part of our individual money management. Compound interest should excite all of us to "pay ourselves first!"

The other day an investment advisor recommended that if a twenty-two year old person would invest two-hundred dollars monthly in 10-year U.S. Government instruments at 8.5 percent, it will accumulate to $815,451.00 by retirement age. Assuming the discipline to invest 10% of our income, whether an allowance or earned income, will establish the habit and with compound interest, provide a handsome addition to retirement. Children can be learning that at five years of age.

It would have been far wiser for the government to have developed a plan back in the thirties, that would have encouraged individual responsibility for investing for retirement rather than the Social Security system that may have seemed quite reasonable fifty years ago (to some people) but has grown to be a monster of an entitlement program in the nineties. If our young people could be free to invest that money, their retirement would be greater.

Unemployment compensation was originally developed to prevent the extremely high unemployment of the depression years. I think, because the employer pays it, the unemployed person figures he won't profit from it, unless he uses it when unemployed. Looking for employment does not become serious until the money is about gone.

That money was intended to be returned to the employer if it were unused, which it rarely, if ever, is. If the amount was included in the employee's gross paycheck and was considered a contribution from the employee, it wouldn't cost the employer any more money than it does now, but would make a psychological difference to both the employer and employee. The employer would not resent the ex-employee using the money instead of looking for employment and the employee would know that it was his to use if needed.

If the amount set aside would be available at retirement if it were unused, it might encourage the person to immediately look for work. If the worker understood clearly that the money would be available for his own retirement, it might be viewed differently. It certainly could enhance his retirement funds, if it hadn't been used, but it would be a life-saver, if it was needed.

Families can help children understand both the value of money and how to use it responsibly. Very young children can learn about investments and the rate of return. Starting a savings program for the family can be a major way towards responsibility for oneself and model money management for our children. Even kindergarten age children can understand money management and investment, if they are involved in the decisions.

The family can discuss the required expenses, such as savings, the cost of the mortgage, insurance, car expenses, and share the decisions regarding flexible spending such as the kind and cost of food eaten, the cost and frequency of eating out, the kind and cost of various recreation activities. It will help everyone feel a part of the family.

In addition, It will be a model for how to share decision-making. Most children grow to adulthood without realistic knowledge of what the cost of living entails or how to share decision-making. The parents will have to learn how in order to model for their children. It won't be such a shock when the children grow up and money and family management becomes their responsibility.

Responsible money management in families and responsible participation in government are two very important ways we can model. It will make a difference in our families and our country.

When only half of our citizens are voting, it indicates that we have not helped our growing populations understand what a vitally important ingredient informed voting is for responsible government. We can demonstrate in our families the value of voting on issues. We can discuss the issues with our children, inviting their input on how to vote, so that our children understand the importance of voting on our country's issues.

We have much to learn about efficient money management. We need to advocate better ways of learning about our political candidates and issues.

All of us can write frequently to our representatives, demanding the elimination of waste and inefficiency, letting them know we care. Children can share in writing.

Both our country and our family *can* live within our means. Assuming the responsibility to do it is a wise decision.

We have been driving our kids crazy because we have not been financially and politically responsible.

We Drive Our Kids Crazy With the Negative Power of Television

"My toddler is blinking terribly. He shakes his head in rhythm with his blinking. Do you have any idea what can be the matter?" was the request of a distraught mother. I asked if she had talked to a doctor.

"Oh, he couldn't find anything at all. He just said to watch him to see if I could discover what it could be," the mother replied.

A few weeks later, the same mother came in with a relieved report. Her children had been watching Sesame Street. As she passed the kitchen doorway, she noticed that her little one was nodding vigorously. Because the doorway was directly in line with the children and the television beyond, she observed that the nodding matched the movement on the screen. Fascinated, she carefully checked her initial perception.

She stopped all television viewing and within a week the blinking and head shaking had stopped. She also said that the whole family was more relaxed, had time for other activities, and didn't have the number of squabbles that often invade family life. Best of all, no one missed the TV.

Many children are spending more time watching television than time in school. It has been stated that preschool age children are the largest viewing TV audience with some children spending one-third of their time watching whatever is on, since many people just leave television on all day. Television does have a hypnotic effect.

It is important to know that television viewing generally encourages passivity not knowledge. What children are *not* doing is important.

They are *not* relating to people. It inhibits talking. Language development is a major part of the preschooler's development.

They are *not* acting out what they are learning. Play is children's work and is extremely important. When children play house, for example, they are acting what they are learning about moms and dads, families, activities to keep families intact. Playing house is a very important childhood activity.

Children are *not* physically active; climbing, jumping, running, skipping, hopping, all movements essential for healthy physical and mental development.

Neurological development is not well understood, but a study by physicians, found there was an increase of hyperactivity since the beginning of Sesame Street. It was found by comparing doctor's files with before and after the beginning of Sesame Street in different parts of the country. Not necessarily a well-conducted scientific study, but, certainly, suggesting a relationship.

Sesame Street was developed so action would move quickly in order to keep children's attention when normal household activities might grab their attention. Often it is not the child that is excited about watching Sesame Street, but the parent who believes it is important. They program the child to watch regularly.

Organized subliminal messages are supposed to be forbidden but we all learn from many kinds of experiences and television sends many messages. For instance, many children's programs undermine respect for adults.

The recent movement for schools to accept television equipment in exchange for news programs with commercial messages is a current controversy. It has a much more important message than each individual commercial.

Four Arguments For The Elimination Of Television was written by Jerry Mander, an advertising man who became disturbed by the power of advertising. He states that it is an invasion of the mind which expects to alter behavior, alter people. "One person, the advertiser, invades, millions absorb. A deep, profound and disturbing act by the few against the many for a trivial purpose." "The medium *is* the message" according to McLuhan.

Children are *not* participating with people, *not* involved in decision-making, *not* resolving conflicts, (except which program to watch) *not* learning positive attitudes toward emotions.

TV is isolating, eliminates conversation, often takes the place of reading stories.

Imagination is creating our own images, inner picture making, creativity. Television provides the images and discourages imagination.

Problems on TV are solved easily within a half hour, often through technology or drugs, if not drugs during the show, the commercial interruption will often emphasize drugs. Such programming does not aid in the necessary decision-making and problem-solving processes that are essential to communication among people.

By offering "adult" programs late at night, it is assumed children will not be watching. However, according to one study, there are probably more than a half million children viewing television between twelve and two AM.

Television merges the differences between adults and children. Advertisers picture children involved in many adult activities, such as clothed in designer clothes and jeans eliminating any distinction between adult and child behavior. Offering deodorants for seven to twelve year old children is the most recent example.

"Do you want to be the stinkiest child at the party?"

Children are learning their history from television and it is not accurate. History is adjusted to improve the chance for good ratings. Here in Spokane, plans to show a movie about Kevin Coe, the local convicted rapist, is causing concern because it is not an accurate portrayal of what actually happened.

Accurate history is too necessary for an understanding of the world to base our knowledge on stories adapted to television.

Sex-role stereotypes are fostered, Blacks and Indians particularly. One small Indian was frightened when his parents dressed up in traditional

Indian clothing with the elaborate head-dresses. His ideas about Indians came from watching cowboy and Indian shows where the Indians were the bad guys.

Might makes right is a subtle but powerful message. Low tolerance for the frustration of learning is another unhappy result. The students want passive entertainment rather active involvement in figuring out solutions.

Juvenile crime has increased 1600% between 1952-1972. At that time, violence was not associated with television, but more recent research is making a connection. With the increase of violence in society, it is blurring the distinction between what is real and not real, what is moral and not moral, unspeakable crimes and normal feelings.

Parents *can* control the amount of television children watch, if they believe they should. Children who have a rich social life with lots of interaction with other children and adults, and many interesting creative activities, don't choose to watch much television.

Dorothy Cohen, an early childhood specialist, believes the years between birth and five years of age are so important that this age child should *never* watch TV. When so much learning is taking place during these early years we must provide a rich learning environment. Children learn by doing. Passive watching of television dulls the genius in each of us.

I have mixed feelings about Saturday morning viewing. If mom and dad will use that time for husband-wife courtship purposes, I am for it. With the VCR and planning, discriminating choices for children to view would be more appropriate. Healthy food without sugar that won't make a mess (like Cheerios) will give mom and dad some mighty important time alone together. This is also a vital part of successful family living and is difficult to arrange during these hectic times.

Another area of concern is the health aspects of spending time in front of the television screen.

John Ott has spent a lifetime researching the impact of light on plants and people. He has found that the different kinds of light have a major impact on plants and people. The electro-magnetic field of such things as electric blankets, which people are in close contact for quite a length of time, can be detrimental. Pregnant women, in particular, are being advised not to use electric blankets. Manufacturers are advised to change them. Power wires are, also, under belated investigation. Word processors, microwave ovens, and TV monitors are under suspicion. There appears to be measurable impacts on the health of people.

When classrooms have been changed to have full-spectrum lighting and window glass, the behavior of children in the classrooms becomes calm and relaxed. There is much more we need to learn regarding the impact of differing kinds of light on our health.

Criticism and evaluation of television is legitimate. We need to know what it is doing to us. Sitting in a semi-darkened room with little interaction with other humans and only two senses operating, staring at light for hours and hours is definitely a form of sensory deprivation. The mental images are not personal. I wonder if this can be considered brain washing, paving the way for "Big Brother".

I have not addressed the serious problem from the standpoint of the kind of news and information we are getting and who is qualified to make the decisions. With one to three minute "bites", we are not getting the kind of information necessary to know what is happening nor to be able to make informed choices when voting.

The increase in the many problems I addressed in the introduction may be directly related to the developing influence of television.

Television may be driving our kids crazy as much as we are.

We Drive Our Kids Crazy Unless We Respect Our Own Personhood

WHOOPEE!!! I was walking on air as I left the Sunday School class. I had been the only person in the class that had known the quote the minister wanted. Again, WHOOPEE!!!

As I was driving home with our children, I suddenly came down to earth. Puzzled, I wondered why that had made me feel so very good. After all, I was a college graduate, I had been a teacher before I was married. Why, oh, why was I so impressed with knowing the right answer. I even remember the quote, "The mills of the gods grind slowly..."

I didn't figure out the reasons at that time.

Years later, when our children were older, I became a Director of Parent Education at a community college. A young mother who was enrolled in our first toddler program helped me to understand what had happened so long ago.

She had been the supervisor of student teachers at a university for eight years. At this time she was staying home with an eighteen month old infant who was challenging her with her "no's". As we learned about toddlers and, more generally, explored parenthood, I put my experiences and her experiences together and made an exciting, illuminating discovery.

Her husband was treating her very differently as a stay-at-home mother, than he had when she was an administrator at a university with an impressive income.

Suddenly, she had become "just a housewife" and someone to wait on him. His parents had come from the "old country" and he was reverting to that traditional image. His young wife had been reduced to a "go-fer". After all, she had *only* one small baby to care for now so she could do all the work at home. It was the change in his attitude toward her that was so disconcerting, (although she had not consciously recognized it as such.)

Suddenly, I had connected her experiences with that emotional "high" that I had experienced so long ago. There was a definite connection between my "high" and her depression.

The world "out there" does not respect mothers who *just* stay home and baby sit. After all, anyone can baby sit. Without any qualms, we get our eleven year old next door neighbor to come in to baby sit. It is believed that housekeeping does not take any special talent, although some forward-looking colleges are recognizing the value of such experience. A mother who stays home with her children and keeps house is about as well respected as a "go-fer". That "whoopee" excitement of twenty years before had reinforced my lost self-esteem as a person with intelligence. Without understanding the dynamics involved, I had internalized the powerful just-a-housewife message from the world "out there", even though I loved being a wife, mother, and homemaker.

When I was middle-aged, there was a depressed time and my builder-husband had difficulty getting work. He asked me to return to teaching so that he could get his teaching certificate. In order to renew my teaching degree, I was going to have to return to college. Going to a university after twenty years away from the classroom was frightening for me to contemplate. There was no alternative, so I enrolled. It was amazing to me to discover that I could easily compete with those young kids.

The state had just approved funds for preschool for children with disabilities which was to be my first teaching position. It was a satisfying challenge. I couldn't believe it when the director brought university professors out to watch me work with the children.

Gradually, I was regaining the self-esteem I had lost as "just-a-housewife".

I was exhilarated when I connected my insight with what was happening to this young mother. I believed I now understood how I could make a difference. I hadn't understood what was happening when I was young, but as I pondered the puzzle, my experiences and this young mother's experiences came together in an inspiration direct from heaven.

The young mother was depressed because she was feeling that she had lost her personhood by the change in the way she was being treated. Her husband, without realizing it, was reverting to the "normal" male role. I, suddenly understood the impact of those powerful messages, silent as they are.

I invited one of the college teachers to come speak at our parent seminar when both moms and dads would be there. I chose this person because he was so very masculine-looking, with brawny, muscular body, dark beard, deep voice. I asked him to speak on the importance of being a person and the difficulty of doing this when one was just-a-housewife. I felt the dads would identify more easily with a male person saying this.

The need for the feminine movement grew out of the general lack of respect for "women's work". When I am always someone's wife or someone's mother I lose my sense of identity. The speaker emphasized the importance of having a time to be your own person. He described how he took their two boys shopping every Saturday, taking most of the day to do it. He would have the children help him look for each item, learn to read the name on the package, help him push the basket, look for something special to take their mother. His wife knew she was free for most of the day, so she could take a bubble bath, a class, read a book, sunbathe, whatever *she* would like to do for herself.

In the beginning, the young husband asked questions in an antagonistic way. Gradually, he became less defensive. By the end of the discussion, his question indicated he was beginning to understand.

He did understand. It was fortunate he did. This young couple had not wanted to wait another eight years for a second child, so they had put in for adoption. One month after receiving a brand new infant boy, they discovered she was pregnant. She said that she so appreciated the change in her husband. He was very helpful in many ways and she knew that she could not have made it through those busy months without his support. He even mopped the floors.

It reminded me of one of my cousins. He was an eye, ear, nose, and throat specialist. He always told his wife that he couldn't boil water so that he would never have to fix his own breakfast. I wondered how he could become a doctor if he couldn't even boil water. Just so, we have been manipulated through the centuries.

Just recently, we were talking in our family about this need to be a person. It is easy to get caught up in your job, housekeeping, marriage, and parenting roles. My husband, reflecting the traditional male role, commented that our youngest daughter was able to get away from her job, because she went to her husband's basketball games. We said that didn't count. Then he said that she was expecting a baby. We said that didn't count either. No matter how much we might enjoy watching our partners' activities, no matter how excited we are about expecting new babies, it doesn't fulfill the need for our own personhood.

As I mentioned in the chapter on religion, when I was young, I couldn't understand Christ's admonition to "Love your neighbor as yourself." I thought it was selfish to love yourself. You were supposed to love others. I had to grow up to learn that I can't love my neighbor, nor my husband, nor my children, unless I love myself. I cannot love myself unless I understand the need for being my own person. Because I am *me*. Then it is possible to truly love others. Then we can unselfishly put the needs of others ahead of our own.

It is extremely easy to lose sight of the need to *"Know Thyself."* That takes time.

Recently, a national-level official made news headlines because he called his secretary, Little Miss Coffee-maker. He defended it as an "endearment". Another official publicly referred to "wetbacks". It is difficult to always hide what we think. If we think about it, we can enumerate many stereotypes that cloud our thinking and prevent recognition of people with their rights to personhood.

"Mothers don't do that!" exclaimed a baby sitter when a mother admitted that she let her child climb to get things out of the cupboard. The mother in our parent group was reacting to that baby sitter's stereotyped perception of what a mother is.

I can remember the shock I experienced, after our first baby was born, when I realized that I did not *feel* like a mother. I had expected to become an "all-knowing" mother. I had expected to "feel" like I thought a mother would "feel". I didn't feel any different. I wondered how I was going to know what to do with this brand new baby, if I didn't feel like a mother.

Recognizing the importance of preserving or regaining our personhood is a primary condition if we are to be either a good wife or a good mother, a good husband, or a good father. I have to love myself in order to love my neighbor. Unless I respect my personhood, I will not respect yours. Learning to treat our children as people with their own rights to personhood, treating them with total respect is essential if we aren't to drive our kids crazy.

My "mothering" changed a great deal between our older children and our younger children. I had learned to trust our younger children. I don't remember when Stacy was put in charge of her going to bed and getting up time. She was eight when our daughter-in-law met us. She was so impressed because Stacy went to bed without reminders. Our oldest daughter was a mother when our youngest daughter was a teenager. She reminded me that when she was in junior high school, I was reminding her.

"Nancy, it's your bedtime." I would say nightly. "But, mother, I have to finish my homework," would be one of her excuses.

"You knew your bedtime, you should have started your homework earlier." I did not understand what she was really saying.

"Mother, I am old enough to be in charge of my bedtime!" I should have listened. By the time Stacy arrived, I had learned much.

I assumed far more responsibility than I should have and undermined her personhood.

Life was much more pleasant when I had learned to respect personhood and allowed the younger children the freedom to become responsible.

It is easy to look at our new babies and believe it is up to us to shape them into what we want them to become. It has been compared to what a sculptor does to stone. Comparing the child to a seed and the parents to the gardeners who will provide an environment where the seed can grow into its full potential is more appropriate. We don't try to turn a rose into a rhododendron.

I am not going to be able to provide that environment unless I recognize my own personhood and respect my right and responsibility to maintain that personhood.

I have to believe that it is important for me to grow to my full potential, before I can provide the freedom for others to achieve their full potential otherwise I become controlling and dictatorial or ineffective and passive.

That doesn't necessarily mean going out to get a job. It does mean evaluating our priorities, the essential material needs, each partner choosing to work shorter hours so that there is ample time to share with our children.

Flexible scheduling for employees must become a reality. After all, it is essential for business and industry to help make our children's environment wholesome, since our children are our future.

The amount of money earned, has been a measure of worth for too long.

A group of young women, who were educationally disadvantaged, had been tested by the employment agency and assigned to vocational programs based on the results of the tests. The ones that received the lowest scores were assigned to the child care class and I was to teach them. When they arrived in class they were so upset, because they believed that anyone could babysit.

They surely hadn't signed up to go to school to learn how to baby sit.

The first thing I had to do was to convince them of the importance of child care, that this was the most complex, rewarding challenge of all.

If one wanted to be a clerical aide, one could be taught to type, and with practice one could become an expert typist. What they did as a typist wasn't going to impact the future.

We didn't have a formula for child care, but it was the most important task mankind had. Even the "experts" had not been able to develop a formula that would guarantee successful child growth and development. It would take a great deal of knowledge about child growth and development, patience, creative thinking, and sensitivity to understand and provide what children need.

It was that group of young women who helped me understand what successful teaching entails. When the class was completed, one young woman gave me the greatest compliment of my teaching career and verbalized for me what good teaching needs to be and that it is possible to do.

"Mrs. Payne, I have learned a lot in this class, but do you know what I think is the most important thing I have learned?" Of course, I waited with interest, not expecting the wonderful insight she then shared.

"That we are to care for children, the way you cared for us." I was stunned at her insight! I was impressed with both her and me! I was not consciously aware that I was giving that message, but I realized it was true. That is what learning takes. That is what Bloom proved with his emphasis on the affective environment. I always learn more from my students than I ever give.

Providing what children need, is the greatest gift we can give this world. We have said that we put children first, but it is not what we say, but what we do and we are driving our kids crazy.

What I am trying to say is that choosing a way to provide a warm supporting comforting fun family life can be the most challenging choice of all and may be the way to develop our own best *personhood* in the process. One has to be a very strong person to become the model that our children need in order to develop their own potential.

It is when we feel guilty, that we are challenged to find a way to overcome the problems in order to alleviate the guilt. When we take the pressure off our children and return it to our own shoulders, we won't have to feel guilty about what we are doing to our kids. We will quit driving our kids crazy.

I am proud to be me, I like me, I will take time to grow as a person, then I can do *anything*. Becoming the parents our children need is the greatest, most satisfying challenge of all.